Diary of a Bishop's Garden

One Year in the
Garden at Rose Castle

Janet Queen

Bookcase

Copyright Janet Queen
First edition 2009
ISBN 978-1-904147-46-6
Published by Bookcase
19 Castle Street, Carlisle, CA3 8SY
01228 544560 Bookcasecarlisle@aol.com
Printed and bound in Great Britain by
CPI Antony Rowe, Chippenham and Eastbourne

For Joan and Tam

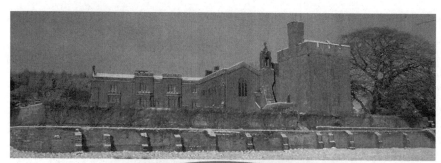

4

CONTENTS

North-west View of Rose Castle by Samuel and Nathaniel Buck, 1739

A photograph of the Dutch garden as it appeared
in the mid-nineteenth century

Preface

When I first arrived at Rose Castle in the summer of 1995, I was captivated by the stateliness of this red sandstone property, its picturesque setting amongst fields above the Caldew river, and the aura of timelessness I felt when walking round the garden and grounds.

Over a period of eight centuries, the castle has evolved to its present form, and the garden and surrounding grounds have evolved along with it. Historical records concerning the castle's garden are scarce. There is little documentation about garden layout, crops cultivated or plants grown for ornamental use. Even more elusive is information on the many gardeners who have tended this ecclesiastical site for hundreds of years.

It is not until the early 1700s that a glimpse of the garden's past is revealed in detail when William Nicolson, the 45th Bishop of Carlisle, records lists of plants that he brings to Rose Castle from the Royal Botanic Garden, Edinburgh.

It was while holding Bishop Nicolson's notebook in my hands that I decided, as a working gardener and former student of the Royal Botanic Garden, Edinburgh, I would like to keep a notebook of one year's work at Rose Castle garden. The period between August 2002 and August 2003 that I have chosen to document falls almost exactly 300 years after Bishop Nicolson was writing about the garden in his own notebook.

While gardening at Rose Castle, I have worked closely with both Bishop Ian Harland and Bishop Graham Dow. After fourteen years, I find I am even more enthralled by my surroundings.

In producing this diary, I hope to transmit my deep affection for the garden and provide some detailed information that may be of interest to those who tend this garden in the future. But most importantly, I hope to capture the nature, spirituality, history and beauty that combine to form such deep, natural tranquillity in a garden where bishops have walked since the thirteenth century.

Rose Castle - An Historical Introduction by David Weston

Rose Castle stands in a secluded rural setting about seven miles south-west of Carlisle, in the county of Cumbria not far from the Scottish border. The land on which it stands was given by King Henry III in 1230 to Bishop Walter Mauclerc, the fourth bishop of the Diocese of Carlisle which had been founded by King Henry I in 1133.

The oldest surviving parts of Rose Castle date from the mid-fourteenth century, after earlier buildings on the site had been burnt by the Scots. The gateway and adjacent mantle wall and part of the north range of the castle give some idea of its appearance at that time. A plan of the castle dated 1671 and an engraving of 1739 usefully depict later stages of the castle's development. At its most developed stage, it was a massive defensive fortress built round four sides of a central courtyard. There is evidence that in Tudor times its defensive qualities were reduced by the introduction of some large windows in its outer walls. This became an issue in the Civil War when it was attacked, captured and burnt by Parliamentary troops in 1648.

At the restoration of the monarchy and the Church of England in 1660, a new bishop of Carlisle was appointed who began the process of rebuilding. However, the decision was soon reached to rebuild only two sides of the castle giving it its present L-shape. The rebuilding was initially in the classical style favoured in the late seventeenth century. This can be seen in the 1739 print of Rose Castle, which shows how it must have looked in 1745 when a Jacobite raiding party came but in the event went peaceably away. In the early nineteenth century, Bishop Hugh Percy re-imposed the newly fashionable Gothic style both outside and inside the castle. As a result of all this, Rose Castle has that mixture of styles which, while dissatisfying the purists, provides a fascinating insight into its long history.

The only significant change since then, involved the demolition of another section of the building in the 1950s to make the castle more compact and better suited to continuing use by the bishops to the present day. The building provides domestic accommodation for the bishop and his family, his office and offices for his staff, the chapel, accommodation for guests, visitors and retreatants, and rooms suited for meetings and large-scale hospitality. Rose Castle stands in extensive gardens and grounds, which are the subject of this present work and which contribute to the tranquillity which is its distinctive quality.

Canon Dr David Weston lived and worked in Rose Castle when he was chaplain to the Bishop of Carlisle from 1989 – 1994

AUGUST

Lupin seedpods crackle. They spring open to release and propel their burnished seeds as far as possible from the herbaceous border. In the late morning heat, shades of purple, lilac, silver and white look resplendent against the east-facing sandstone wall. Along the whole length of this wall, cream and white blooms of the climbing rose, 'Madame Alfred Carrière', form a lightly fragrant summer backdrop. In the languid summer air, when every sound and movement is greatly exaggerated, it is possible to follow the path of the flying lupin seeds on their hopeful trajectory. Many of them disappear down into the moat below. Designed to protect Rose Castle from intruders of ill intent during bygone eras of warfare and unrest, the moat was originally a deep, fetid, dank bog. Now, the gently contoured hollow of the moat shimmers in a tranquil summer haze of beige and golden grasses that conceals its turbulent past.

Perhaps in future years, lupins escaping from the herbaceous border may eventually manage to establish themselves between the sturdy, sandstone buttresses that flank the moat, but at the moment, the grasses there form an undisturbed canvas of glowing colour and subdued, rippling movement throughout late summer. This morning, as lupins sizzle, the castle's guinea fowl pick, peck, chirp and chatter contentedly through the long grass, disturbing small groups of shy goldfinches that flit and cavort amongst the stalks of ripest grass seed.

Looking back, I think my fascination with potatoes began when I worked in Scotland in a Perthshire hotel garden during school holidays. As the only girl employed among the other seasonal gardeners, I was often chosen for jobs requiring, according to the head gardener, a gentle touch. Lifting early potatoes that were to be sold in the garden shop or taken to the chef was a routine job, but lifting potatoes for exhibition at the much revered, annual village flower show was altogether a different matter. These potatoes had to be exactly the same size with eyes arranged in a recognisable pattern and skin unblemished and unbroken. We were looking for five examples of perfection from each variety, destined to be laid out on a white paper plate and scrutinised by judges and local villagers. A first prize promised not only a mention in the local newspaper, but also ultimate respect for the head gardener from other gardeners in neighbouring Perthshire properties and estates. While the boys set out in the morning with mowers and hedge cutters, the head gardener and I deftly and slowly worked along the drills of potatoes, gently forking the tubers to the surface where they would lie in the sun until midday to dry. The damp, musty smell from the moist, delicate skin of newly dug potatoes is one of the sharpest memories of my early gardening days.

Now, over twenty years later, in this Cumbrian castle's vegetable garden, I grow a selection of about twenty varieties of potato. My own interest in this subject also happens to have a practical and welcome outcome – a supply of potatoes for the castle and also for people who have contributed to the garden. Three more varieties, more obscure than others, are about to join the collection. They were obtained as tiny plants last June and grown on in pots in the cold frame: 'Shetland Black', 'Salad Blue' and 'Highland Burgundy Red'. With careful watering and protection from slugs, each plant produced a few sizeable tubers this year. This morning I stored them away safely in wooden boxes to await next spring's planting season.

We discovered the ashes just before midday. Edging and hoeing in the vegetable garden is one of summer's pleasures; an hour each day maintains the sharp formality of the small, rectangular and square beds. At lunchtime, on my way from the vegetable garden to the cottage, Jim met me and asked if I would walk with him to the gatehouse. Just beyond the gravel parking area at the gatehouse, not far from a young walnut tree we planted in winter, lay a silvery grey shape of a cross on the woodland floor, shaded by a yew tree from the August sun. Last week, the bishop had mentioned the request from the son of a former bishop's butler that his ashes might be scattered in the grounds of Rose Castle. There were few other details, but we knew the butler's son had grown up at the castle and wanted to return to the place he knew and loved during his childhood. Nobody here saw the ceremony take place. The discreet and simple cross was sprinkled like frost in summer over low-growing grasses and fragments of yew bark and pine cones.

On Wednesday, Thursday and Friday mornings, I collect the newspapers for the castle and cottages from a wooden box tucked inconspicuously behind one of the sandstone pillars at the entrance gates of the castle. The bishop's chauffeur attends to the other days. In the early mornings, my walk up the drive beneath mature, stately trees, including two *Sequoiadendron giganteum*, is always a pleasure – even in the darkness of winter months. This drive may not be as long, grand and sweeping as many castle entrances, but the narrow, tarred road flanked on either side by plantings of trees of varying ages is a haven for wildlife. It is uncommon not to see bullfinches, treecreepers or woodpeckers, or perhaps the hare that has been resident for a couple of years. In the spring, roe deer have occasionally crossed in front of me, making their way up to the woodland on the hill above the castle. The closely cut carpet of dark

green grass between trees and shrubs highlights the shape and textures of tree trunks, luring the eye to linger on different details according to the time of day or quality of light. In spring and early summer, wild flowers are left to grow as they wish, with mowers restricted to cutting only a strip of grass close to the road sides. Bluebells, primroses, red campion, ragged robin and cow parsley grow in the grass between the trees and are then allowed to set seed before being cut in July. The combination of wild flowers, trees and shrubs of varying ages, and grass maintained at different heights throughout the year, is probably why the castle drive provides sustenance for so many birds.

On his arrival, the bishop expressed his fondness for soft fruit. Blackcurrants, redcurrants and gooseberries were already growing in diverse areas of the garden, but it seemed more practical if we could grow all the soft fruit in one area; it would also look more attractive. We decided to establish a fruit garden that would be productive and easily maintained, and as it is an area that is overlooked by several castle windows, we felt it should have an air of formality.

Symmetrical rows of currants, gooseberries, raspberries and rhubarb are now separated by grass paths that are wide enough to be cut by a small tractor mower. At the most southern end of the fruit garden, the soil is particularly heavy and tends to remain damp throughout the year. A few cranberries are growing there, and after two years, each plant has produced a considerable amount of berries. This afternoon I took several cuttings; the sooner this awkward area is filled with cranberries, the better. It is a useful plant for soil that most fruit would find inhospitable.

The prospect of growing strawberries in this part of Cumbria is not a naturally occurring thought in the minds of local gardeners; high humidity, wet summers, and an overpopulation of voracious slugs are the precluding factors. This summer, against all those odds, a raised bed with about twenty plants of 'Red Gauntlet' provided a large crop of juicy, sweet berries. Some fruit did succumb to mould and rot, but we were surprised at the success of this tentative, first attempt. Netting the bed was essential; blackbirds were easily outwitted, but some berries were still lost to early morning raids by one of the peahens. After jumping on top of the net and forcing it down with her weight, she was then able to reach through to the fruit. Fortunately the bishop's chauffeur lives in the cottage overlooking this part of the garden so he is able to chase the errant peahen whenever she is spotted near the strawberry beds.

Today, just before a shower of rain, I planted another raised bed with twenty rooted runners originating from the existing 'Red Gauntlet' plants so that, by next July, two beds should be fully productive. Strawberries are due to become a feature of Rose Castle summers.

It was a pleasure to be asked to judge flowers and pot plants in the horticultural section at the local show. It was obvious from the competition entries that this summer's weather has caused much trouble for gardeners. Freshly picked dahlias were spattered with droplets of soil splashed onto the perfectly formed blooms by this morning's rain. Pansies had not escaped nibbling by slugs, and the sweet peas were blemished from too much rain and wind. These detrimental elements may spoil the flowers in the vases on the show bench, but they do not manage to dampen the spirits of those taking part in the competition. It was heartening to see so many entries. As a judge at a show, I am expected to look for perfection, uniformity and high standard of presentation. Three flawless, velvety-red, pom-pom dahlias had to win the prize for best exhibit from all categories, but had I not been wearing my judge's badge, a vase of rather wild, wind-blown, tousled herbs would have been my personal choice.
While casting an eye over the excruciatingly long parsnips, giant onions and scrubbed beetroot on the vegetable bench, it passed through my mind that I could perhaps exhibit a selection of my potatoes next year – not for competition, but as a Rose Castle contribution.

Tonight, I was the only person on the property; the bishop and his wife are on holiday, and the chauffeur and his wife are also away. After locking up the castle, Jim set off over the border to a hotel in Gretna to begin another evening's entertainment - music for brides and their wedding guests.

There will be few nights here when the castle, garden and grounds exist in such solitude. Just before darkness fell, the sky celebrated the drawing to a close of the warmest day of summer. Shades of turquoise and pink formed the background colours for a golden moon with its misty, amber halo. I walked out to the silent, grassy expanse at the front of the castle, to the site of long-dismantled turrets set into the thick wall that was once necessary for the protection of the castle and grounds during unsettled times. Bats flickered close to my face, owls called to each other, hedgehogs shuffled and rustled through dry, copper beech leaves. I could not help thinking how the peacefulness enveloping the castle this evening contrasted with these infamous years of belligerence and strife: both Robert the Bruce and Edward I were involved in the darker, more unpleasant history of the castle. Although it was late, a few unsettled rooks were creating a noise in the wood to the west of the castle. Their sporadic, ungainly calls were the only interruption in the stillness of the night.

In the white and purple border, clusters of button-shaped flowers of *Achillea ptarmica* 'The Pearl' were glowing with a brilliant luminosity. An idea for a new planting came to mind: Rose Castle's moonlight border - an indulgent planting, to be viewed when the moon is full and the skies clear. Over the years, I have noticed the luminescent qualities of certain orange or yellow flowers, especially nasturtiums and *Bidens*. This vision of a border of flowers, lustrous and resplendent in moonlight, with large, silky moths flitting around night scented stock and fragrant lilies, accompanied me on my walk round the garden.

When I reached the vegetable garden, I looked across to the small-paned windows of gardener's cottage brightly lit up from within. They contrasted with the black, solid silhouette of the nearby castle. Like a magpie in the night, I immediately noticed the tiny mirrors sewn into Indian wall-hangings, glittering and sparkling like jewels through the windows.

The sound of lawnmowers is urgent and continuous throughout the day and into the evening. Preparations for the arrival of guests for the bishop's birthday celebrations this weekend are the main consideration. We desperately want the garden to look its best. The top lawn takes up most of our day. Usually cut once a week throughout summer with a ride-on mower, the grass here has never been an example of perfection, but it does assume a generally well-maintained appearance. This weekend, however, the lawn is required by the bishop and his guests for croquet. Cutting it two or three times in the same week with the small cylinder mower is the only way we can achieve a smooth finish, removing the worst of the tufts, lumps and bumps so the croquet players will be unhindered. At the end of the day when we stand back to admire our work, the castle seems to rejoice in the pleasure of this perfect foreground of manicured, striped, green velvet. This is how it should be, especially as it is overlooked by the bishop's office – we make a decision to dedicate some extra time every week to maintain the lawn to this standard, but unfortunately it is not a promise.

When I first put a bow over the strings of a half-size violin to produce some shaky, grating notes, little did I realise the seeds were then sown for a lifetime of playing Scottish dance music. Traditionally, Scottish gardeners and foresters often had musical abilities; historical documents can be found in the archives of estate offices relating how gardeners and domestic staff provided music in castles and 'big houses' for dances. In every culture you can find strong links between music and working on the land.

Although conventional venues such as halls, ballrooms, mansion houses, hotels and castles provide the usual setting for dances, at times I have played with bands in more obscure settings: a ranch on the MacKenzie river in Oregon, a L'Orient street party in France, and a chicken shed in Aberdeenshire.

In the past, Jim and I have provided informal music in Rose Castle for small gatherings, but this evening's ceilidh in the wooden-floored dining room was our first organised event. The band was a simple line-up, but one we considered suitable for a small party: side drum, bodhran and fiddle. Three of us were dressed in medieval costume, the lights were low, and we stood in a line at the end of the dining room overlooked by 18th century paintings of the castle. MacPherson's Lament was the opening tune before we launched into dances including Gay Gordons, Cumberland Square Eight, and Strip the Willow. We had warned the drummer that it would probably be a short night, but the bishop and his wife set a frenetic pace for the dancing. The floor remained full, long into the night. The final dance was an Orcadian Strip the Willow with a set the length of the room, played at speed and danced with enthusiastic whirling abandon. It was designed to finally deplete any remaining energy on the floor, but it felt as if it could continue forever.

As the walls absorb the music, it is hard not to let the imagination wander with distracting thoughts while wondering who has played

here during hundreds of years of bishops' gatherings and celebrations. Perhaps in the same room, some of the castle's long-departed gardeners played versions of the same tunes we played tonight.

Now that summer is fading and there are unlikely to be large groups of visitors to the garden, I lifted the onions that had been left in place purely for cosmetic reasons. This damp summer has not been favourable to onions, but clearing the onion beds leaves a surface of bare soil and I know it is much more interesting for visitors to see beds full of thriving vegetables. The onions are laid out to dry in the greenhouse, and as I bind them together in uncouth bunches, I imagine long, perfect pleats of shining, red and golden onions hanging in the castle kitchen. At this time each year, I remind myself to find someone to teach me the art of stringing onions together in true French, ornamental style.

SEPTEMBER

Two young *Buddleja x weyeriana,* planted in the spring and
delighted to escape the confines of their pots, celebrated their
freedom with a summer flurry of lush growth that is now bending
beneath the weight of clusters of small, apricot and cream-coloured
flowers. By late afternoon, when the heat of the day's sun has been
absorbed by the south-facing walls of the gatehouse and orchard
borders where the buddleias are planted, butterflies find the
combination of sunshine, heat and flowers irresistible. This
afternoon, as peacock butterflies gathered lazily on nectar-rich
flowers, I took a few close-up photographs capturing details of the
vivid colouring of their wings against the subtle, sunrise shades of *B.
x weyeriana* flowers.

Redolent of autumn's approach, the musky scent of fresh sap from cut stems and bruised leaves of *Helichrysum monstrosum* is instantly recognisable. In the past, when growing dried flowers in estate gardens as a crop for cutting, I grew them in large groups or long, straight lines. But now, fewer flowers are required and space is limited, so I grow them amongst vegetables or in borders between established perennials. This summer, small clusters of *Helichrysum* brightened up the edges of onion beds and will provide height and continuing colour now that the onions have been lifted. This use of annuals amongst vegetables saves the garden from too many expanses of bare soil after vegetables have been harvested. Children visiting the garden are drawn to these brightly coloured blooms; the papery brittleness of the petals is a texture they do not usually associate with flowers.

For drying, *Helichrysum* are best cut in the afternoon of a warm, dry day. I choose stems with flowers that are not yet showing their yellow centres. When dried, flowers with petals that are not fully open tend not to disintegrate so readily. Shortly after lunch, I brought a bundle of flowers into the potting shed, stripped off the leaves, and tied the long stems into small bunches. The familiar *Helichrysum* aroma filled the dimly lit shed and the sticky residue from the sap turned the skin on my fingers and palms almost black. During my first year here, I attempted to dry the flowers by hanging bunches upside down from nails in the beams of the potting shed roof. Although this shed does not feel damp, the flowers became damaged by mould and I realised an alternative method would have to be found. Now, I hang the bunches from the curtain rails of north-facing windows in the living room of our cottage. The flowers dry perfectly and, for two or three months, the windows are embellished with colour.

Harvested earlier in the summer using the same method, *Helipterum* is another excellent flower for drying that is easily grown from seed. It grew contentedly this year between lettuce and radish, but I made sure I planted most at the edges of beds close to the main grass path through the vegetable garden. Eye-catching flowers in shades of pink, with either yellow or black centres, are a favourite among visitors who are at first attracted to their delicate elegance. On learning that this flower can also be dried, some visitors ask me to write down the name and a recommended seed source. Perhaps they will indeed grow it in their own gardens, or perhaps it will remain a memory of their Rose Castle summer visit.

Dried flower arrangements often seem to lack hints of blue. *Delphinium* blossom, picked just before it is fully opened, is ideal for drying, but in the early summer when *Delphiniums* are in full bloom, I am too enthralled with these fluid spires of blue and also too involved in the season of planting and sowing to think yet of cutting and drying flowers. Harvested at this time of year, *Limonium sinuatum* 'Azure' is an indispensable, annual variety of statice for those who are attracted to bright, vivid blues. In the vegetable garden, it is planted as a border around beds of leeks where the blueness of the flowers is further emphasised by the backdrop of tall, metallic blue, leek foliage. This planting combination comes to fruition later in summer. Newly planted statice can be slow to show signs of growth. Rosettes of young leaves lie close to the soil for weeks before any movement is detected. In July, before there were any obvious signs of flower stems on the statice, a visitor to the garden asked me to explain the special relationship between leeks and dandelions as this seemed to be a planting combination that we favoured. She was most embarrassed when I explained that these dandelions were, in fact, statice.

Yesterday evening, after the castle was locked up and the alarms were set, we drove north to Crieff in Perthshire. This morning, our return journey began through dense mist, slowly disappearing to reveal clear blue sky. With time on our hands on a warm sunny day, we decided to take a circuitous route home and travelled down to the south-west coast of Scotland. Tucked away in a corner, this is a part of the country I have seldom visited. This afternoon we saw it at its best with a calm silver sea and a wide clear horizon. By the time we reached Logan Botanic Garden, it was bathed in dark golden sunshine and long shadows of late evening. The grandeur of tall *Eucalyptus* and *Cordyline* set a harmonious scene for a garden embellished with all manner of tender plants. Jim describes this garden as 'a botanical zoo'. He does not sharing my enthusiasm for pushing back the boundaries of the cultivation of tender plants.

Being a man who also mistrusts cultivars, he was, however, enamoured with *Dahlia coccinea*. Elegant, copper-coloured flowers were held on tall stems amongst foliage that was much more lacy than the sturdy, heavy foliage of most dahlias. Unlike overdeveloped and overweight cultivars, this species had poise and deportment that did not require unsightly staking. At Haddo House garden in Aberdeenshire we grew dahlias of every colour, shape and height. They filled a long border and were the main supply of late summer, cut flowers for Lady Aberdeen. The tubers were huge and gnarled and, although they had been divided many times by previous gardeners, some varieties had been growing there for at least forty years. At that stage in my gardening life, I did not think of introducing some of the more refined and less gaudy species.

September mornings bring heavy dew on grass that is still lush and full of summer's vigour. This morning a blue sky and sparkling dew vanished without trace within twenty minutes. But the ensuing downpour, continuous throughout the day, offered an excuse in the morning to spend a couple of hours in the glasshouse and potting shed.

Patiently awaiting attention, *Streptocarpus* cuttings that had been taken hurriedly and randomly earlier in summer are now rooted. We have a small collection of named varieties but, because of their fickle nature, especially during winter, it is prudent to keep more than one example of each plant. *Streptocarpus* are ideal for north facing windowsills of the castle, but as soon as they finish flowering, they are

brought back to the glasshouse. Some of the more fussy varieties are overwintered in our cottage where I can keep a close watch on them. While potting up rooted leaf cuttings this morning, I thought about adding a few more varieties to the collection, but space in both the glasshouse and our cottage windowsills is the limiting factor.

I hope never to be without potting shed, rainy days; wooden work-benches, damp compost, spiders' webs on windows, rain falling on a slate roof, and shelves stacked with Victorian clay pots.

This morning, I was picking damsons just after early morning mist cleared from the orchard. Climbing up wooden ladders to reach damsons from the highest branches amidst dappled shade of

yellowing leaves, I knew I was following a long tradition of harvesting fruit as gardeners have done here for hundreds of years. There are few historical accounts of this garden but a photograph from 1911 shows a Dutch garden of intricate design laid out in the site of the present orchard. I doubt whether the oldest trees in the orchard would be any more than around seventy years old. Although the exact situation of the castle's original orchards is unknown, we do know from records that 'apples, pears, plums and other fruits' were grown at Rose Castle in the 15th century. Also, in 1621, there is an account of apples being sent from Rose Castle to Naworth Castle as a present from the wife of Bishop Richard Milbourne to Lord William Howard.

When we first arrived at Rose Castle garden, the existing orchard was used as a paddock for sheep. An area of rough grass with no more than a few mature fruit trees was surrounded with a tangled, barbed wire fence. Most of the trees were damaged and misshapen. Although it was an unsightly and neglected part of the garden, we realised there was great potential for the creation of a productive and picturesque orchard. At that time, the bishop was also keen to upgrade this area. He negotiated the removal of the sheep with the farmer and then a selection of about two dozen fruit trees were planted in the winter of 1996. All of the young trees, including apples, damsons, plums, pears and greengages are now bearing reasonable quantities of fruit.

Last year, the branches of the oldest damson trees were breaking under the weight of their fruit but this year's harvest has been poor. Most of the fruit is collected in buckets for use in the castle, but every year we save enough to make about three demijohns of damson gin. Damsons soaked for three months in a mixture of gin and sugar slowly release a rich, red pigment from their dusky, purple skins. The result is a luxurious, sweet liqueur. While picking damsons, I look forward to the richness of colour and fruity taste of damson gin by a wood fire on a cold, rain-lashed, midwinter night. But in the depths of December, it takes only one glimpse of this rubescent liqueur to recall scenes of sunny, late summer, orchard mornings.

Rose Castle's geographical situation is convenient from many points of view. Its equidistance between the south of England and north of Scotland means that most locations throughout the UK are within reasonable reach. Friends travelling long distances often decide to break their journey here, staying overnight and setting out early the next morning. Head gardeners from Scottish gardens are our most usual visitors, on their way to collect or deliver plants, or to visit other gardens. The head gardener from Inverewe Gardens on the north-west coast of Scotland arrived last night. Plants, gardens and gardeners were the topics of conversation until midnight. Professional gardeners are inescapably linked and entwined with gardens of their previous employment, gardeners with whom they have worked, trees they have planted, plants they specialise in, estates where they have lived. This intense network of stories, species, secrets and speculations must have been in place ever since gardeners lived and worked at historic properties.

As we walked along the white and purple herbaceous border on the terrace above the moat the next morning, our visitor remarked upon the delicate, sweet scent of slightly decaying, late summer, rose foliage. Between 1827 and 1856, Bishop Hugh Percy commissioned the well-known designer and horticulturist, Sir Joseph Paxton, to plan the layout and planting of the terraces and rose garden. So far, no details of these designs have been found, but we assume the site of the present white and purple border would have been included in these plans. No hints as to the whereabouts of Paxton's rose garden have ever been uncovered. We are not keen on recreating the past; there is no need to do this at Rose Castle garden, but an insight into previous plantings and designs would be interesting.

Throughout summer, the castle's office windows are often open in the afternoons. Old climbing roses entwined with sweet peas provide a framework of blossom and scent. Earlier in the season, *Lilium regale* adds an extra intensity of fragrance that hopefully finds its way through the open windows. At the moment, silky pink, *Cosmos*

flowers are held on tall stems, well above windowsill height. *Verbena bonariensis* grows far too tall and straggly here, but I planted one or two, anticipating how the secretaries would appreciate the butterflies it would attract at this time of year. Along with the indulgence of experimenting with tender plants in this sheltered area, I am trying to entice flowers, foliage and fragrance to grow against and tumble through open windows - or at least, to create the illusion. Work in an office must be so much more pleasant when a garden reaches out to you from beyond the windows.

September sunlight cast its translucent, amber veil over the garden throughout this month. Soil crumbles, beechnuts crunch underfoot and roses are enticed to flower again. The overcast, cold, damp days of spring and early summer are excused. *Rudbeckia* flowers are abundant and unblemished, their strong stems standing tall and straight. Large, daisy-shaped blooms with petals in velvet shades of mahogany, rust, and dark yellow are backlit by the sun. Other late flowering perennials are flourishing too, many looking as perfectly formed as those you see in plant catalogues. No blustery, end of summer, equinoctial winds arrived this year to spoil their poise and symmetry. Still blooming profusely, sweet peas, surrounded by white Cosmos to disguise their scrawny, lower stems, seem to float like jewels around a barely visible, metal obelisk.

Beds that contained peas, broad beans, onions and early crops of lettuce are now awaiting their annual supply of organic matter. This job continues throughout winter, but with the soil being so dry and friable just now, I could not resist making a start today on the most awkward beds containing soil that tends to become compact and poorly drained in wet summers.

OCTOBER

First thing in the morning, Jim set out with a mower and strimmer to the moat but returned to the potting shed within half an hour. Ordinands who are staying in the castle for a few days had come out to pray in the peacefulness of the morning and were sitting on wooden benches Jim has placed in particularly picturesque areas of the garden. Determined though he is make use of every dry morning for grass cutting, Jim decided the sound of machinery would destroy the tranquil ambience of the bishop's garden, especially as it was being appreciated in such a time-honoured way.

It was a perfect October morning. On the hill above the castle, the first hints of autumn colour were beginning to become noticeable on the line of sycamore trees that borders the larch wood. Cattle walked slowly past the garden wall through wispy patches of mist on their way to the fields by the river. On the other side of the wall, ripe pears were hanging like golden lanterns from old trees that were once espaliered. Sunshine and warmth throughout September have ensured this year's fruit is sweet and juicy. Their yellow skins are tinged with shades of pink, and although some of the pears are cracked and blemished, the flavour is not diminished in any way. Some branches still retain hints of their original, lateral training against the wall, but most trees have an upright, free habit. At one time, these pear trees would have been carefully shaped and tied into the east-facing wall - definitely a morning job for the gardener who would have relished the heat of the early sun on his back. Decades have passed since these trees were so diligently tended and now the most we can do for them is to prevent them from growing too tall above the wall. They have the potential to cast too much shade onto the garden at Gardener's Cottage, especially the area where we eat out during warm summer evenings.

The head gardener from Crathes Castle in Aberdeenshire, Scotland, spent last night here. He was on his way to a conference on maples at Westonbirt Arboretum, and Cumbria was a suitable place to break his journey from Aberdeenshire. We were students together at the Royal Botanic Garden in Edinburgh and also went to the same school in Perthshire. He brought a plant he thought we might like for the garden here at Rose Castle: *Magnolia sinensis.* At the moment, I am undecided about where to plant the it. I may put it near the gatehouse where it can be enjoyed in future years by visitors to the castle who do not have time to walk round the garden. We do, though, have a policy not to plant anything too close to the gatehouse. The walls are so old and squint and full of interesting nooks and crannies - it seems a pity to obscure such intriguing details. The south-facing side of the building is probably a better choice, offering shelter and protection from cold winter winds.

This year, the border of shrub roses, planted by one of our predecessors, relished the combination of the early summer's high rainfall and the late summer heat. Although not the best year for rose blossom, lushness of growth has resulted in an unruly, dense tangle of wayward stems and foliage. *Convolvulus,* or bindweed, has always been a problem in this border and was even more difficult to control this year as it wound its way around the framework of strong, healthy rose stems. By the end of September, each rose seemed to blend into the growth of its neighbour, linked by the twining stems and heart-shaped foliage of bindweed forming a sea of green along the whole length of the border. There are so many jobs to do in summer – some things always manage to go their own way.

A knee-high box hedge separates the rose border from the grass path. After pulling away the bindweed and pruning the roses this morning, gently shaping them back to individual, distinguishable specimens, I then trimmed the box hedge. The air was filled with the strong, spicy aroma of the sap released from cut and bruised foliage of *Buxus sempervirens* 'Suffruticosa'.

Rosa 'Scharlachglut' required the most vigorous pruning. Its long, bold, upright stems seemed intent on growing as tall as the top of the wall at the back of the border. In full bloom in July, this rose is captivating. Petals of large, single, dark red flowers appear to be fashioned from velvet. In flower, it is a most luxurious and sophisticated rose, but in growth habit, it is wayward and unrefined. Unruly stems, however, are easily curtailed at this time of year and the beauty of the blooms more than makes up for its fleeting, flowering season.

In keeping with the ecclesiastical theme at Rose Castle, *Rosa* 'The Pilgrim' nestles close to the bottom of a flight of stone steps at the other end of the border. Tame and subdued in growth, it forms a rounded bush with large, perfectly symmetrical, double flowers with neatly arranged petals in a clear, soft shade of yellow. In the garden we expect yellow shades to be warm, hazy and sunny, but the flowers of 'The Pilgrim' are sharp and almost icy in their yellowness. Of all the roses, this one gathers most compliments from visitors.

The white and purple border that is at is peak in early summer holds on to a little late colour with the help of *Echinacea purpurea, Verbena bonariensis, Cineraria maritima*, several lilac *Aster lateriflorus* and a few white *Allium*. Most of the foliage of earlier flowering plants is beginning to fade. I am never keen to begin clearing herbaceous borders until there is a drift of seed heads and browned foliage and not a flower to be seen. The problem here is the upright, long shoots of the climbing roses on the wall behind the border. By this time of year, they have now grown well above their allocated height and are clearly visible from the bishop's offices. They look like an unkempt, straggly fringe clambering over the top of the wall - a sight that is exaggerated on windy days when they blow around in further disarray. Now that the lawn outside the offices is neatly cut and manicured, Jim is keen to cut back the roses to complete the scene of linear orderliness.

Before the climbing roses are pruned and clippings drop down over the wall onto the white and purple border, it is best if I can work my way along cutting back the foliage of plants that are preparing for winter while leaving those that are still flowering. It was the perfect morning for this job; a drying wind through the night left foliage dry

and easy to work with. Previous autumns have not always offered
such propitious weather for this work - nothing is worse than cutting
through the decaying, mushy foliage of a rain-soaked border. Soil in
this border is once again in desperate need of attention. Three years
ago I forked in large quantities of leaf mould along the whole length
of it, but today as I cleared mounds of foliage, I could see and feel
the airless, compact, heaviness of the soil. I made a note to give this
border priority when it comes to allocating my valuable leaf mould in
the winter.

By the end of the day, the climbing roses were tamed. In the evening,
we looked back at Rose Castle from the distance of Rose Bridge, and
the straight outline of the top wall was now clearly visible.

The first rainy day for a month. I filled a barrow with onions that had been laid out to dry in the cold greenhouse and brought them round to the shed. It took most of the day to sort and clean them. It may sound like a monotonous job, but I enjoy peeling away the dusty outer layers to reveal smooth, shining surfaces – especially the rich, claret shades of red varieties. By mid-afternoon, the onions were organised into green, mesh bags, ready for storing. One bag of onions was taken over to the castle kitchen for immediate use but the rest will be stored in a shed in the yard to keep them cool so the bishop's wife can use them throughout the following months.

The removal of the onions from the greenhouse leaves the bench almost bare apart form a few pots of chilli peppers. The seed catalogue warned me that the variety 'Heat Wave' probably would be the hottest chilli I could grow. It was right. They are so hot nobody will use them. The long, curled, red and green peppers look so attractive on the plants, but this year, their function is purely ornamental. The compost heap will be their destination. Next year, I will make sure I choose a mild variety.

Tomatoes are grown in the other half of the cold greenhouse. For many weeks of the summer we thought they would never ripen, but September's unexpected sunshine gave us a reasonable crop. The chauffeur's wife will make chutney from the remaining green tomatoes, and after they are picked and the plants are on the compost heap, the greenhouse will be empty for the winter months.

Early this morning, there was a dusting of frost across the garden. In the distance, and clearly visible from the upstairs windows of Gardener's Cottage, a snake of white mist followed the contours of the Caldew river. Fallen, heart-shaped leaves from the four poplar trees bordering the lane to the cottages were scattered on the mossy tarmac. Later in the day, the combination of dampness and sunshine released a bitter-sweet scent from the yellow leaves – an autumnal scent that belongs to poplars alone.

The white and purple border has been receiving a lot of my attention this week. I am working my way along it, forking it over and removing the roots of perennial weeds. Ground elder has been bad this year, but at least the long, white roots are easily seen and can be removed with little resistance. Problems arise when they become tangled and enmeshed in the roots of plants. A patch of blue bearded iris has become terribly riddled with ground elder and couch grass. In the summer, I can disguise the pernicious presence of ground elder by pulling off the leaves as soon as they appear, but although it may not be immediately noticeable to visitors to the garden, I always know it is still there lurking beneath the surface. Today I decided the only remedy was to lift all the iris, pick the weeds from between their rhizomatous roots, remove every fragment of weed from the soil, and then replace the iris. It was a long, slow job, but a pleasure to be working with the warmth of the sun on my back.

While I was forking soil and picking out weeds, flocks of mistle thrushes fluttered amongst the trees in the moat woodland. They were feasting on the fleshy, red berries of the yews – I counted at least forty thrushes flying across the grassy moat to the woodland where they all landed in the one yew tree with much undignified fluttering and clamour.

When I had replanted the clean and weed-free area of border with equally clean iris, I found I had a large number of plants left over. We decided to plant them along the edge of the globe artichoke beds. Blue flowers against silver foliage is always an attractive combination, and as the artichoke beds are south-facing and quite freely draining, it seemed to be the best option.

I rarely work my way through beds and borders in the autumn and winter without adding copious amounts of organic matter. I usually have a choice of leaf mould, dung from the farm or compost from the garden heaps. This year, I am making use of a pile of shredded, well-rotted walnut branches.

Three years ago, an old walnut tree near the gatehouse was damaged in winter winds and was left leaning precariously across the road. It was a sad day for us when the tree was felled but it had to be done. Most of the wood was chopped into logs for firewood and the smaller branches were shredded. In time, the large pile of wood chips slowly darkened and decomposed into a much smaller heap. Each year, this mature tree produced an abundant crop of walnuts, and some years they were even sweet enough for us to eat. Pheasants, red squirrels, peacocks and guinea fowl would spend hours foraging beneath the tree. Apart from the nuts, the tree supported a vast array of insect life that also attracted wild birds in great quantity. Walking past this tree, you would always glimpse fluttering wings high in the branches or hear rustling amongst fallen twigs, dried leaves and nut shells. Not far from where the tree was felled, we planted a new, young walnut as a continuation of species traditionally planted in the grounds of the castle. Hopefully, many years from now when it bears crops of nuts, there will still be such a thriving population of red squirrels and other wildlife at Rose Castle.

The soft and powdery compost that has formed from the shredded branches seems to be an excellent soil conditioner. After forking in generous quantities of the compost between the plants in the white and purple border, the soil now feels more open and manageable.

Just as it became light this morning, I filled a bucket with some flaked maize and stale bread and walked through the frosted grass of the orchard to the little enclosure where the six geese spend most of their time. They have access to a small stream so they always look impeccably groomed and clean with shining, white feathers. By October when grass growth begins to recede, the geese are thankful for some extra food. I am always greeted with much flapping of large, white wings and a deafening cacophony as they

rush towards me as soon the wooden door from the orchard to the paddock is opened.

This afternoon's garden visit for about fifteen people from the Whitehaven area had been booked several months ago. As soon as the visitors stepped from their cars, my eyes glanced at their feet. Fortunately, this afternoon was sunny and dry, but damp grass can cause considerable damage to suede shoes and summer sandals. I think most visitors expect gravel paths or paved surfaces, and are often not prepared for our more rustic, grassy routes through the garden. Today's visitors, however, were determined not to let any footwear problems spoil their walk round the garden. The late afternoon sun cast a low, beguiling light across everything it touched. There was a lot of interest in the white and purple border, especially in the area that I had been working on lately. Everyone wanted to know what I had been forking through the soil to make it look so organic and healthy. Ornamental gourds also provoked much conversation. This year, I have been growing them in a corner by Strickland's Tower, named after Bishop Strickland who was resident at Rose Castle in the early 1400s. Now that the foliage of the gourds is dying back, their warty, yellow and green fruits are quite visible. One lady was so transfixed by them that it seemed only natural to give her a couple to take home.

As part of garden visits, we unlock both doors to the tower and show visitors around the first two floors. A few years ago we found a dead squirrel inside, so the bishop installed a mesh door that could be closed over the wooden outer door whenever it was open to prevent squirrels and swallows from coming in and becoming trapped. Fitter and more agile members of the garden group are welcome to go all the way up to the top of the tower if they choose. The spiral staircase, thick sandstone walls, and stark simplicity of the tower capture the essence of times gone by. With bare wooden floors, candlelight and a roaring log fire, Jim and I, along with a couple of friends, have enjoyed meals in the tower on a few occasions. A wooden trestle table and rustic seats set the scene for these winter feasts. We cook the food in the kitchen in Gardener's Cottage and carry it over to the tower. With no electricity, and the only source of heat being the open fire kept ablaze with hardwood logs, the tower has been the backdrop to some of our most memorable meals.

On a cloudy day, the north-facing, gatehouse border can be a rather cold and disheartening place to work. The soil tends to be heavy and wet, and the area close to the red sandstone wall of the gatehouse is

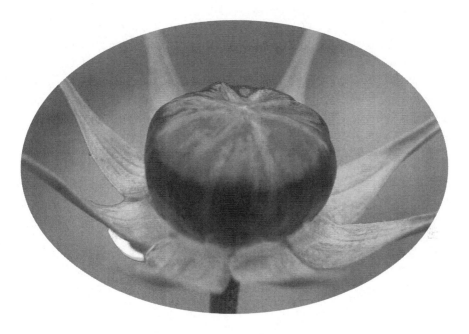

bereft of sunlight throughout the year. The mature and majestic
weeping willow, just to one side of the gatehouse, thrives in the
moisture retentive soil.

Today, there was not a cloud to be seen as rays from the early
morning sun danced around the gatehouse. Spiders' webs were
highlighted in the pale, golden light. Leaves from the weeping willow
floated to the ground through the silence of the blue-skied morning.
Every detail of the outline of the building was dark and clear against
the sky; hundreds of years of history and secrets locked away in the
red sandstone. So many people, many of historical eminence, have
passed through the gatehouse archway on their approach to the castle.

The moisture-loving perennials that form a dense covering of foliage and flowers from late spring until autumn at the gatehouse suddenly become a little wild and unkempt in appearance as they collapse and fade at this time of year. Plants thriving in this border include *Euphorbia griffithii*, *Geranium phaeum*, *Dicentra spectabilis*, *Ligularia przewalskii* and various varieties of *Hosta*. It is a whole day's work to cut back the foliage and then fork a generous quantity of leaf mould through the soil, but on this last day of October, amidst an autumnal celebration of golden leaves and sun, there was no better place to be.

NOVEMBER

For the next few months the gatehouse border will rest beneath the darkness of its rich, leafy, damp soil. In May the scene will be transformed; sunlit, white, pointed petals of one hundred 'White Triumphator' tulip flowers will float above clumps of emerging perennials. The tulips were planted today, randomly positioned throughout the border to provide a natural effect.

On the other side of the wall, Jim was burning branches from a yew tree that had to be removed to prevent overcrowding in the moat woodland. As I planted tulips in spaces between established plants, wood smoke snaked and swirled through the archway of the gatehouse. Without a breeze to cast it away, the aroma of burning yew lingered in the damp air around the garden all day. It is unusual for us to remove a yew from the garden, but this one had

grown from a self-sown seedling and had, unfortunately, settled in a place that would allow it only a short life. In the afternoon, the largest branches were sawn into logs that, when fully dry, will burn for many hours in the castle's winter fires. This is the time of year when the bishop's woodshed is filled until hardly a space is left for a single log. As wood is used, we replenish the store with logs from winter's casualties, usually fallen limbs collected in the mornings after windy nights. Winter work always involves some pruning or crown-lifting of mature trees - another useful source for re-stocking the woodsheds.

At first light this morning, a mosaic of yellow and russet leaves from lime and beech trees decorated the black tarmac of the castle drive. They lay as they had fallen through the night, not yet scattered aside by the postman's van. A red squirrel was rummaging through mottled oak leaves searching for acorns. Walking down the drive after collecting the newspapers, I could see the promise of a dry day from the clear, open sky.

Coffee time on Tuesday afternoons around three o'clock in Gardener's Cottage is a sociable affair when there is a gathering in the kitchen. Discussions, stories, jokes and laughter mingle with the aroma of freshly ground coffee. It is on Tuesdays that we are lucky to have extra help in the garden from a young man who works here on a voluntary basis. His association with the garden began when he was a horticulture student at the local college where his tutor happened, by coincidence, to be one of my former classmates from the Royal Botanic Garden, Edinburgh. As part of his horticulture course, this young man came to Rose Castle twice a week for practical work experience. Although he now has his own gardening business, he returns to Rose Castle every week if he is not too busy and joins in with whatever work we happen to be doing at the time. His help is greatly appreciated, especially in the early summer months when grass cutting is an essential part of the daily routine. If the bishop's chauffeur is not driving on a Tuesday, he also helps out in the garden. It means that there are four of us available to make lighter work of jobs that would normally require much more effort for fewer hands.

As years pass, strands from the web of contacts established at the Royal Botanic Garden, Edinburgh, continue to thread through my life. As young students, when plant and botanical knowledge was our main focus, we were perhaps unaware of the influence, help and pleasure this intricately woven structure of friends and acquaintances would bring us in later years.

Unbeknown to us, when Jim and I first arrived here, links between Rose Castle and Edinburgh Botanic Garden were already in place.

Three hundred years ago, Bishop William Nicolson received a delivery of plants to Rose Castle from his friend, Mr Sutherland, the first Regius Keeper of the Royal Botanic Garden, Edinburgh. This list of plants is recorded in a calf-bound notebook in Bishop Nicolson's own handwriting. Three-hundred-year old pressed flowers, almost transparent with age, casually nestle between the yellowing pages. Bishop Nicolson was a well-respected botanist and naturalist, and he noted the wild flowers, shrubs and trees he saw while walking or riding. A later publication of his notebook provided the first comprehensive Flora of Cumbria. The names of

plants and their habitats are interspersed with fascinating, everyday comments that give us an insight into the day-to-day life of a bishop in the late seventeenth and early eighteenth centuries.

Although the notebook contains only two lists of plants he describes as being 'set at Rose', Bishop Nicolson could never have known that his botanical notes would become, centuries later, one of the few remaining historical reports of plants cultivated within the grounds of Rose Castle. Detailed below, his wry account of taking delivery of the plants leaves us wondering what other specimens might have been included if the carrier had been of a more trustworthy disposition.

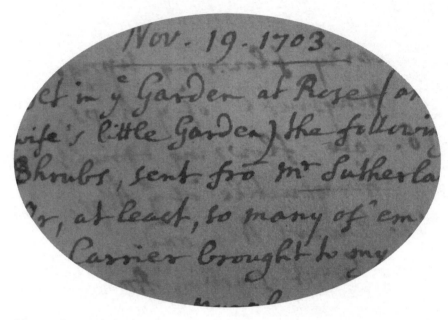

November 19ᵗʰ 1703
Set in the Garden at Rose (and my wife's little Garden) the following Shrubs, sent from Mr Sutherland; Or, at least, so many of 'em as the Carrier brought to my hand.
Deep purple Lilac
Dwarf Medlar
White Beam Tree
Rose without Thorns
Yellew Rose
Buck (t) horn-Tree
French Tamarisk
German Tamarisk
Sea Buck-Thorn
White flower'd Lilac

Mock Willow
Upright Honey-suckle
Wayfareing Tree
Shrub Trefoil
Early-flowring upright Honeysuckle of the Alps
Late-flowring upright Honeysuckle of the Alps
Dwarf Almond
Sweet-smelling American Rasp
Shrub St Johnswort
Curran with Gooseberry Leaves
Persian Jasmin
White Pipe Tree

There is still some research to do on this list before we can decide with certainty which plants Bishop Nicolson was referring to. Some names are almost identical to common names we use today, but others, such as White Pipe Tree or Mock Willow, are more obscure. Long winter nights are ideal for spending time trying to unravel the descriptions used three centuries ago.

The second half of November continues with damp, blustery days. Frosty nights have turned remaining foliage in the vegetable garden to shades of brown and black. The dusty blue leaves of leeks and the dark green vitality of spinach are the only visible remnants of summer's burst of growth.

In theory, the soil is probably now too damp and heavy to work, but months could pass before ideal conditions arise for digging the vegetable beds. In Cumbria, where rainfall is fairly high, one has to be prepared to cast aside the rule book and take an opportunistic approach, otherwise much of the work would never be done. Drainage is a problem in the vegetable and soft fruit gardens. The soil here tends to be naturally heavy, but I expect the lack of drainage may be a result of the routine use of a rotovator that was part of the winter and spring regime in the garden long before we arrived. As a consequence, the formation of a solid, impenetrable layer beneath the soil surface now hinders natural drainage. There are times, after prolonged rainfall, when it is impossible to work the soil in the vegetable beds for days, no matter how opportunistic one feels. In the days of the rotovator, the vegetable growing areas comprised three large, rectangular expanses of soil. During our first few years here, we gradually transformed those areas by creating a more ornamental design of small, raised beds with grass paths between them. On completion, there was little need at Rose Castle for the rotovator that then lay redundant in one of the gatehouse sheds.

At that time, I was making regular advisory visits down to the gardens of the bishop's palace at Bath and Wells and I knew how much the gardeners there desired a rotovator to help them cope with their large vegetable garden. It made a lot of sense, therefore, to organise the transportation of our rotovator down to Bath and Wells where it would be, once again, fully utilised.

This morning, I drove to Penton to visit the rhododendron nursery at Penton Mill. The owner has recently returned from a plant collecting expedition to China, bringing home seed from many rare species, some of which will be completely new to cultivation. In the style of a Victorian plant hunter, he has now completed at least ten plant collecting expeditions to areas that are generally considered inaccessible to Europeans. The stories of mountains and plants are

fascinating. He delights not only in the wonderfully diverse and rich floras of these countries, but also the cultural and social aspects. This rhododendron collection, maintained by himself and his partner, is now one the most unique in the country. My visit today was for the purpose of gathering information about his latest plant collecting trip – it is an ideal winter topic for my weekly gardening column in a local newspaper.

Perhaps Rose Castle garden may host a small collection of these rare and unusual rhododendrons some time in the near future. Inspired by the garden at Muncaster Castle, I have often visualised a planting of tree rhododendrons on the bank that slopes steeply from the narrow path running along the north wall down into the moat woodland. At the moment, the bank is smothered in a thick layer of brambles and perennial willow herb, and every so often, we set about clearing small areas to allow space for the large ferns that struggle tenaciously through the prickly, snaking bramble stems. I imagine standing in the lowest area of the moat woodland in May, looking up towards a canopy of rhododendron blossom with a background glimpse of the castle's red sandstone crenellations. The view from the top of the bank would be equally entrancing when looking down through twisting, rust coloured stems of tree rhododendrons rising above a carpet of newly unfurled fern fronds. So much could be made of this bank, but it is difficult to allocate time and energy to this site when more conspicuous areas of the garden need our attention. With a long term view of eventually cultivating the bank, *Cercidiphyllum japonicum* and *Davidia involucrata* were planted four years ago at the side of the path running along the top. *Davidia* is one of Jim's most admired trees, but the *Cercidiphyllum* was planted for its colourful autumnal display that would be particularly eye-catching when viewed from the bishop's bedroom window. It will be a few years before it is tall enough to fulfil its purpose, but each year, the heart-shaped leaves show distinct tinges of pink and red in autumn. The *Davidia* has been much more reluctant to establish itself. Apart from producing a few leaves, it showed little sign of movement over the years and appeared obstinate and unwilling. Just when we had almost given up, it burst into life this spring with the growth of a strong, healthy leader stem at least eighteen inches long. These specimen trees are now in place, growing healthily, and awaiting further development of the bank.

A dry morning after a night's heavy rain is the ideal time to rake leaves. Crisp, brittle, dry leaves are a joy to walk through, but when attempting to rake them up and collect them in a wheelbarrow, they

are far too flighty and unruly. Wet leaves are heavier to handle, but far easier to control. Carpets of vivid autumn colour on the castle drive have now subdued to shades of dark brown. Narrow strips of grass bordering either side of the castle drive are kept closely mown all year round, providing a contrast with the longer grass beneath the mixture of mature and young trees. The oaks and the sweet chestnut in the drive are reluctant to finally let go of their leaves, but all the other trees are standing bare and sharply outlined against the early winter skies. At this time of year, leaves lying on the grass strips are raked up and taken to the leaf mould heap. This keeps the approach to the castle tidy and orderly, but also, and perhaps more importantly, ensures the continuation of the perpetual supply of soil conditioning leaf mould that I spread on borders and dig into the vegetable beds.

Raked leaves are barrowed to the heap that lies amongst the trees and shrubs about half way down the drive. Grass and leaves have been collected here for many years – long before we arrived. Although so close to the drive, it is a secluded site, and visitors to the castle have no idea of its existence. A curved enclosure, formed by the evergreen foliage of laurels and holly, and nestling beneath the canopy of lime and beech trees, is a shaded, damp haven for the production of leaf mould. We keep the laurels neatly trimmed with the hedge cutter, with the result that this area now has the appearance of a small amphitheatre – unknown to those who pass along the drive, apart from occasional deer, squirrels and pheasants foraging for acorns and beechnuts. The leaf heap area is divided roughly into two sections with fresh leaves kept apart from the previous year's leaves. Ideally, the leaves should have two years to decompose, but they are usually barrowed down to the garden by the end of the first year. Plants certainly do not seem to suffer any detrimental side effects from this only partially rotted leaf mould. Collecting leaves is my main occupation throughout the last two weeks in November, and once the edges of the drive have been cleared, I gather up as many leaves as possible from beneath the mature trees in other areas.

When the small, unheated glasshouse is cleared of tomato plants and bunches of ripening onions in October, the door is left open so the four peafowl can use it for dry shelter during the worst of the winter weather.

A friend who lives not far away at Raughtonhead, regularly joins us for morning coffee. He works as an artist and drummer, the same drummer who played with us in August at the bishop's birthday party. Instead of driving, he sometimes cycles or walks here, using the footpath from Rose Bridge. If walking, he is accompanied by his newly acquired terrier, an endearing, good natured, rust coloured dog. This morning he arrived earlier than usual and was looking for us in the garden. As he passed the glasshouse where the peafowl were settled, there was an immediate, frenzied furore and flapping of wings as soon as the fowl caught sight of the terrier. The birds have had previous experience of small dogs and are extremely wary of them. The mayhem that ensued resulted in one shattered pane of glass and a couple of others being cracked, but fortunately none of the peafowl was injured. Our friend was extremely apologetic while the terrier assumed an air of pure innocence. The fowl will have to endure a draughty glasshouse until we put in a few new panes.

The last working day of November brought with it a good omen for next season. The arrival of a well-maintained, second-hand mower this morning will replace the ailing grass-cutting machinery that has been the cause of so many problems during the summer. This ride-on mower is a professional machine that should be robust enough to withstand the quantity of work required from it during the grass-cutting season, and we hope it will make garden maintenance less labour intensive.

DECEMBER

It is about four years since the grass edges on the drive were cut and reshaped. December is usually set aside for digging the vegetable beds and forking over and mulching the borders, but so much rain has fallen lately, especially through the nights, that working with soil has become impossible. Taking a wheelbarrow through the garden leaves snaking indentations on the paths where the tyre sinks down into the soft, wet, muddy layer beneath the carpet of grass. There is little point in trying to work against the weather, so anything to do with soil is unthinkable just now. Cutting edges on the drive, however, is an ideal job for times when wetness engulfs the garden. It is also one of the most satisfying midwinter jobs because the results remain intact until the spring. Replacing a ragged, undulating edge with a sharp, straight line brings instant formality. Along the drive, grass edges have slowly crept across the tarmac where they have blended into the roadside with a bright green, mossy layer. This natural look is not unattractive, especially beneath the tree-lined part of the drive, but perhaps there should be a more formal appearance, especially closer to the castle.

Few people are inclined to walk round the garden at this time of year so we feel it is worth making the effort to ensure that areas close to the castle, including the gatehouse and front lawns, are given extra attention. I spent most of the day cutting the edges of the drive from the farm cottage down to the gatehouse. The resulting straight lines highlight the quaintness of the gatehouse itself. This building, suffering much damage in times of warfare, has endured many bouts of partial destruction, rebuilding and alteration over hundreds of years. As a result, it stands slightly askew and worn, but exceptionally attractive and ornamental in its soulful asymmetry. Turf resulting from the reshaping of edges is usually stacked in a heap in our cottage yard where it slowly breaks down to provide us with a useful source of loam for potting compost, but today I used it to fill in the holes in the grassy area opposite the gatehouse which were gouged out by the walnut tree when it was felled in October.

We keep this area roughly cut in the summer months, but with its close proximity to the castle entrance, Jim has been keen to give it a finer appearance. With the arrival of the new mower, that is now a possibility in future years. The yew tree in this area is a favourite morning haunt of the four peafowl. It is also the tree beneath which the butler's ashes were scattered in the summer. While the combination of realigning edges and taming rough areas of grass is a gesture to formality, the retention of a balance between pristine maintenance and the naturalness of surrounding, sylvan beauty is something that is never far from our minds.

The bishop and his wife left early in the morning while it was still dark. The narrow borders outside the castle offices were extremely lush and floriferous this summer; the secretaries sometimes had to reach out of the windows at the height of the season to cut away some of the foliage, to allow more sunlight to reach their desks. The best time for tending these beds is when the bishop is away for the day. I am quite sure the clattering of spades and forks in a metal wheelbarrow, and the sight of gardeners bobbing up down outside his office window must be distracting. From spring until autumn, the large rectangle of grass on this level of the garden is regularly mown by the chauffeur or Jim while I maintain the beds, grass edges and gravel paths. From late summer onwards, the plants here require little maintenance, but in November or December, I spend a day or two having a winter clear up which will last through until the beginning of spring.

Although it prefers continuously damp soil, *Salvia uliginosa* thrived this year in one of the sheltered, sunny, window recess. When it was planted in the spring, I hoped its slender spires of sky blue flowers would intermingle with the more sturdy spikes of bright pink flowers from *Salvia involucrata* 'Bethellii' which was planted nearby. It was a vibrant colour combination, and one that lasted until November. Unfortunately, it is not going to be repeated. When tidying up faded foliage and flowers this afternoon, I could see from the spread of the rhizomatus roots that *S. uliginosa* is far too vigorous for this bed. Remaining here for another season, it would soon form a thick mat of roots that would suppress and choke every neighbouring plant. When I find an alternative site where it will have freedom to roam, I will remove it before the end of winter from the close vicinity of *S.* 'Bethellii'. Besides, next summer, I expect *S.* 'Bethellii' will form a spectacularly large plant now that it is established, and there will be no need, or indeed no space, for another plant nearby.

A garden writer who lives further south in the county has donated several plants to Rose Castle garden during the past two or three years. All of them have been grown from seed or raised from cuttings in his sheltered Maryport garden where he specialises in growing rare and unusual plants, many with a slightly tender disposition.

A young *Correa backhouseana* nestles against the wall beside the bishop's office, anticipating a Cumbrian winter while bearing its first dusty, lemon, bell-shaped flowers of the season. *Leptospermum scoparium* is planted close by. These small alcoves beside the windows provide a sanctuary for species with an exotic appeal. Red sandstone soaks up every ray of sun during the day and the walls deflect frosts and provide shelter from the worst of winter winds. Planted out in April,

Callistemon citrinus registered its approval of this site throughout summer with a vigorous display of growth. No red bottlebrush flowers yet, but I am confident they will arrive next year.

Another of his plants, *Hebe* 'Simon Delaux', which has been a great success, was also planted here in the spring. Cold winds in April caused initial problems with scorched foliage, but throughout summer, it displayed rapid growth and vivid, pink flowers. Even at this late stage in the year, there are two remaining spikes of flowers. I hope it will manage to get through the winter – it is planted in one of the most protected sites in the garden.

For the past few days, the garden has been clad in a layer of sparkling frost. Every sound and movement is emphasised in the crisp, clear air.

We can hear the high-pitched, metallic whine of saws from the sheds in the sawmill on the hill above the castle. In the early mornings, water flowing in the Caldew river can be heard from the white and purple border. Wrens flutter amongst the laurels, now much more conspicuous and flighty than they were in the summer.

The top layer of soil in the vegetable beds is frozen solid. The past few winters have been bereft of prolonged frost, bringing instead continuous weeks of dampness. It is hard not to feel that the garden benefits greatly from these dry, freezing conditions. Unhealthy and pestiferous colonies that would normally lurk in wet winter soil hopefully expire as the frost creeps down beneath the surface. It also feels healthier for humans too. Physical work in the sharp air of frosty mornings is hard to beat for imparting a feeling of well-being.

We all met at midday at Armathwaite Hotel for the staff Christmas lunch: the bishop and his wife, the bishop's chaplain, two secretaries, the housekeeper, the chauffeur and his wife, and Jim and myself. After lunch, during which there was much conversation and laughter, we sat for a while with our coffee in the lounge looking out across Bassenthwaite lake. During our drive back to Rose Castle, hills covered with frost and snow were bathed in shades of apricot and lilac as the winter sun cast its light across Cumbria. A large white moon, only one day away from being full, was prominent in the late afternoon sky.

Later in the evening, the combination of thick, white frost and bright moonlight was too much to resist. Around ten o'clock, Jim and I took a leisurely stroll through the garden to experience the beauty of the moonlit, frosted castle garden. Every evergreen leaf of laurel and rhododendron was dusted with a sparkling, glistening layer of frost.

Shadows of leafless trees were cast sharply and clearly on the woodland floor. Along the white and purple border, strengthening arches built into the base of the wall were distinctly highlighted in the silvery glow. All around, silence prevailed, apart from the occasional call of an owl or a flustered blackbird disturbed from its roost.

This morning, I went down to the moat to collect holly. Every year, Carlisle Cathedral receives a few bags of holly from Rose Castle to add to their Christmas decorations. Berries are prolific this year, especially on the variegated holly. Large clusters of shining red berries nestle amongst green and silver foliage, even on the lowest branches that brush against the frosted grass. There are several mature holly trees in the garden and a few more recently planted specimens, including 'Handsworth New Silver'. These young specimens have been planted as replacements for the older trees, some of which look as if they may be nearing the end of their life.

After delivering five bags of holly to Carlisle Cathedral this morning, we returned to Rose Castle to start work in the small wood situated directly to the west of the vegetable garden. During the past few winters, Jim has been gradually thinning the overcrowded trees in the hope that the stems of a few may become strong enough to form long-lived, specimen trees. Counting the rings of felled trees, it looks as if this woodland was planted about twenty years ago. An unusual mixture of sycamore, cherry, larch, Scots pine, cypress and beech have been planted closely together, no doubt with best intentions at the time to maintain the woodland as it developed. But it looks as if the trees were then abandoned and left to grow unattended. Their struggle to find light has resulted in long, thin, weak stems reaching upwards, searching for space in which to spread their branches. With gradual, selective

felling, we hope to give the strongest trees a second chance. Now that spaces are being created between the trees, and the tall stems no longer have the close protection of each other, there is always the fear that they will be at the mercy of a ferocious, winter gale. We just have to hope that they will survive the first few years while their stems strengthen. This small wood has always been an attractive feature, with its flushes of cherry blossom in the spring and bright, fiery colour in the autumn. As it is the only nearby area of established woodland at this side of the castle, we are keen to preserve it. When the newly planted trees in the adjacent field are a few years older, the two areas will blend together.

This afternoon, Jim felled a sycamore. Removing tall, straggly trees from the middle of a densely planted wood is an awkward job. Once it

was on the ground, we chopped up the wood and took it round to the
bishop's shed. Chopping and barrowing was welcome work on such a
cold, frosty day.

While working here, we are always amazed at the large amount of self-
sown, yew seedlings on the floor of this woodland; it is like a yew tree
nursery. Buzzards frequenting the wood on the hill close to the sawmill
ensure the rabbit population has been eliminated from the immediate
surroundings, therefore allowing unhindered, natural regeneration that
is free from grazing animals. A rough wire fence around the wood has
provided protection from cattle and sheep over the years, but Jim has
already started work on replacing it with a wooden fence with a little
gate allowing easy access. This straight, new fence looks so much better
than the loose, rusty wire hanging waywardly from old, squint posts.

Midwinter is brightened with memories of spring and summer, and nothing brings these seasons to mind more than looking through seed catalogues. When preparing seed orders, visions of the garden overflowing with blossom, foliage and vegetables dominate my thoughts. The first draught of this evening's seed order was too ambitious; I know how short of time we are in spring with general garden maintenance, and I also remember the promises I make to myself every spring not to order so many seeds. Priority is given to vegetables and cut flowers grown for use in the castle, but on a rainy, dull afternoon, it is difficult not to be tempted by some of the more unusual offerings in the catalogue. Collating the seed order is one of December's pleasures, especially when accompanied by a blazing log fire and a glass of red wine.

The chaplain invited everyone to his office at three o'clock this afternoon for sherry and home-made mince pies - an informal, end of year gathering. The chauffeur had set and lit the fire in the office for the occasion, and as the warmth from the open fire spread, there was banter between the bishop, chauffeur and chaplain about who should be responsible in future for setting fires in the chaplain's office, now that a solution has been found for chasing the greyness and chill from the room.

I prefer to remember this room when it was the bishop's family living room with ivy tapping on the windows and thick velvet curtains. On my very first visit to Rose Castle, tired from the journey down from Aberdeenshire, I fell asleep in here on a soft sofa, while Jim discussed the prospect of being employed as the castle's gardener with the bishop in his office.

The castle staff are now on holiday until the beginning of January. Apart from spending Christmas Eve in Perthshire, we will be here at Gardener's Cottage to feed the peacocks, guinea fowl and geese during the holiday period. There is no work planned for the garden and grounds over Christmas and New Year. Winter plans, however, can be upset by unpredictable events. On Boxing Day night, three years ago, ferocious gales swept across Cumbria, causing a huge cedar tree at the front of the castle to blow down. Along with the chauffeur, we ventured out into that wild night. As the full force of the storm whirled and raged around us, we saw large limbs torn from trees and debris flying around. It was safer to retreat inside. The next morning there was a scene of terrible chaos throughout the grounds. The first job was to clear fallen tree limbs from the drive so there was access to the castle.

As I walked through the dawn to collect the castle newspapers on the last day of the year, an owl flew onto a branch of a beech tree that forms part of the canopy over the castle drive. In the silence of the morning it remained motionless, apart from the barely perceptible tilting of its head as it looked down to follow my progress with curiosity. Beneath the trees, I noticed the first signs of snowdrops - the tips of foliage only just barely visible.

JANUARY

Frost has seeped deep into the soil. The ground is dusted with a layer of white that is broken only in places where the afternoon sun blackens the soil surface before the frost regains its territory at dusk. The peacocks and guinea fowl take badly to prolonged spells of temperatures that barely rise above freezing. The cedar tree at the front of the castle protects them from the worst of the cold at night when they are roosting on the sturdy branches, but occasionally I have seen them fly down at dawn, their backs glistening with a covering of frost. For the past few days, they have been spending daylight hours beneath the yew trees beside the gatehouse. The dense, evergreen canopy of the yews must provide them with the best protection from the bitterly cold air.

Wood smoke wafted towards the front of the castle throughout the afternoon. The soil may be frozen solid and unworkable, but the crisp dryness of frosty days is ideal for burning piles of branches and brushwood that have arisen from months of pruning and general tidying throughout the garden and grounds. The biggest fire beside the gatehouse will burn for several days and nights.

A wooden door with an old, worn, rusty latch separates the glasshouse from the potting shed. The small windows of the north-facing shed are dusty and cobwebbed, and often at this time of year, covered in iced, silver and white swirls of frost. Cool and shaded in the summer, the shed is bitterly cold throughout winter with the exception of the days when we light a fire. As soon as a fire is glowing and flickering in the hearth, the potting shed seems to develop magnetic qualities, tempting neighbours, workmen and castle staff to venture in. Over the years, there have been many cups of coffee and much conversation by the potting shed fire as rain, hail or snow falls outside.

On the other side of the shed wall there is a south-facing, lean-to glasshouse. Warming rays of sunlight that reach it in the early hours of summer mornings arrive much later during short, midwinter days. A small heater ensures it is always frost-free during winter nights. The main function of the greenhouse is for raising young plants grown from seed in spring. We also keep a selection of pot plants, including about twenty *Cymbidium* orchids, for decoration purposes in the castle. Although purely functional, the glasshouse looks exceptionally attractive throughout most of the year, mainly due to a vigorous *Passiflora caerulea* that has claimed the whole expanse of the whitewashed wall as its territory. From spring until autumn, the wall is clad in dark green foliage, and by the time summer arrives, long, twining stems grow out across the green netting that is suspended across the glasshouse roof to protect young seedlings from scorching sunlight. With jungle-like aplomb, slender stems then begin to dangle down from the roof, each one adorned with three or four exotic passionflowers, so that when you walk through the glasshouse you brush against a cascade of foliage and flowers. The exuberance of this plant sometimes becomes overbearing for such a small area and its vine-like growth has to be pruned to prevent it from becoming too dominant and shade bearing. To keep it under further control, it is cut back quite severely in winter, but tackling the *Passiflora* is a full day's work requiring ample space and creating much disruption and mess along the way. This morning, I removed all the pot plants from the glasshouse and put them into the potting shed to leave myself plenty space in which to work. The tangled, intertwined network of *Passiflora* stems were cut back to the main framework of the plant against the wall. Dusty, brittle fragments of faded foliage and flowers tumbled down around me, eventually carpeting the floor of the glasshouse and the wooden benches. Some stems, although brown and desiccated, are reluctant to be removed and require a lot of tugging and force to loosen the secure grip of their tightly wound tendrils. When the job was finished, the floor swept and plants replaced, winter light flooded into the glasshouse. There is now a sense of restored order and spaciousness.

At first light, the grounds of Rose Castle appear to be encased in a layer of ice. The drive is like a lustrous, frozen river. The castle yard shines like high quality glass. It seems that unusual extremes were at work through the night. A generous shower of rain just before dawn had no time to drain away before it was followed by a sizeable drop in temperature resulting in this morning's glacial landscape. Laurels and rhododendrons droop their leaves in despondent response to the bitter coldness.

Late last night, wild, westerly winds howled around the cottage, rattled windows and blew smoke back down the chimney into our living room. After checking around the grounds in the half-light of the morning, it became apparent that although the wind sounded ferocious and extreme through the night, it had caused only minor damage to the trees; a Portuguese laurel in the moat woodland lost a sizeable branch, and a larger branch had been torn from a pine tree in the drive. I expected a lot worse. While grateful that all our mature trees were still standing, defiant in the aftermath of a storm, I could see the general untidiness that naturally pervades after gale-force winds. There is now considerable clearing up of small branches and wind-blown debris to be carried out in the next few days.

My writing desk is a slender, fold-up, maple and leather relic, said to have belonged at one time to an army officer. Sheltering from this afternoon's heavy rain, I pondered over plant and seed catalogues that were spread out on the polished surface of the desk. Glancing through the window, I could see the results of winter's inexorable march through the garden. The seeds for annuals and vegetables were ordered last month, but my thoughts were now turning to trees and shrubs.

By evening, the completed orders included seed of *Eucalyptus* species, *Arbutus unedo* and *A. menzesii*, *Liquidambar styraciflua*, and *Prunus mahaleb*. *Cupressus sempervirens* echoes my admiration for Italian gardens and landscapes, but the extremely slender form I would like to grow can only be propagated from cuttings.

When we first arrived at Rose Castle garden, I was delighted to see a fine specimen of *Colutea arborescens* growing in a sheltered corner at the base of Strickland's Tower. Unfortunately, it died during a very wet winter two or three years ago and, since then, we have often talked about replacing it. Now, of course, I wish I had collected its freely abundant seed in order to continue the Rose Castle progeny, but even so, there is little excuse not to replace the original *Colutea* with another of the same species. Maintaining planting traditions is good for the soul of the garden. Further south, this shrub is often considered an invasive nuisance rather than something to be cultivated, but it is not so commonly grown in this area. Visitors to the garden always express an interest in it, especially towards the end of the season when it displays attractive, papery seed pods. This afternoon, I found a seed company who listed it in their catalogue, so hopefully a new specimen of this shrub will thrive again at Rose Castle.

Most of these trees and shrubs will have little chance of a healthy life unless they are situated in the most sheltered areas of the garden. This may prove a source of contention. Jim is keen to uncover and reveal as many as possible of the castle walls and surrounding stone-built relics, believing they should be treated as features of equal importance to trees, shrubs and other planting displays. I, too, am just as fond of the ancient masonry, but at the same time, I know the possibilities for growing a selection of more unusual plants, if only the shelter of walls and buildings can be utilised.

The crisp, white petals of the first snowdrop flowers of the season shine brightly amongst subdued winter colours beneath a lime tree in the drive. In the bog garden, winter heliotrope, *Petasites fragrans*, fills the air with the sweet, fragrance of vanilla. The appearance of January

blossom is a cheerful reminder that winter must eventually lose its fight. Both plants grow only yards apart and are brave to display their blooms at this daunting time of year. Yet this unfettered bravura is manifested in two very different and successful styles that manage to withstand, year after year, the varying foibles of winter. Snowdrops are so delicate and fragile in appearance, whereas the less deftly formed *Petasites* flowers are borne on strong, sturdy stems. Both, in their own way, defy the harshness of winter.

Clearing the remaining fallen branches from last week's storms depended on the success of the day's bonfire. Set amongst damp and decaying remnants from previous clearing sessions, this morning's young fire smoked and sizzled but showed little real inclination to burst into life. Tenacious persuasion and a supply of dry kindling smuggled from the bishop's wood shed eventually coaxed a healthy show of flames. When the branches were cleared and burned, we then took full advantage of the remaining, eager fire. The pruning of a few lower branches of a nearby *Prunus lusitanica* has been a lingering subject on our never-ending list of 'things to do sometime'. I expect this is a list familiar to all gardeners. These branches had been allowed to overhang the path that runs beside the wall above the moat woodland. Their shapely, pendulous effect had, over the years, grown to become an obstructive irritation, especially when passing beneath with a mower, or on a damp day when drips of water cascaded from the foliage on the slightest contact. As Jim cut through the thick, smooth-stemmed branches with a chainsaw, I piled them high onto the blazing fire. The air was filled with hissing, crackling and bright orange flames - evergreen foliage can always be relied upon for a spectacular bonfire. Looking back towards the re-shaped laurel, I could see sunlight making new patterns between the pale, newly exposed stems. It was not long before late afternoon rain began to fall on the fire, transforming the peripheral ring of ash from silver to black, but not managing to extinguish its deep, smouldering, smoking heart.

I retreated to the potting shed from the vegetable garden after deciding the rain had become too persistent and the soil too sticky. As a result, I sowed the first seeds of the year and set their pots on the heated bench in the glasshouse. Parsley, sweet peas and lobelia are now on their way. If there are any resident mice or rats in the greenhouse, I will know within days; they find sweet pea seeds irresistible and have an organised system of excavating every individual seed from its pot. In December, we do try to get rid of these rodents from the shed and glasshouse areas, but cold weather often entices others to move in.

Three young witch hazels planted last winter in the new woodland are now in full bloom. The plants are completely clad in flowers, the spidery petals unfurling like a yellow haze along each stem. These three random seedlings of *Hamamelis mollis* were bought from a nursery so it is only natural that the colour of the flowers varies slightly on each plant.

Rose Castle shivers. Dry, sharp, icy winds swirl around the garden. The bitter coldness reminds us of Aberdeenshire winters. These dry winds lift excess moisture from the soil, leaving it crumbly and ideal for digging. This opportunity is too good to miss, so during the past couple of days, the digging of the vegetable beds has been given priority. This afternoon, as we spread leaf mould and compost onto the soil, we caught flashes of red and white as a woodpecker worked its way along a dead branch of an ash tree. The sharp, staccato sound of its beak against dead wood was tossed around in the wind.

FEBRUARY

Six young French partridges are nestling amongst straw in a pen in our yard. They were given to us by a friend in Gretna who rears them for shooting. Knowing about the peacocks and guinea fowl living within the grounds of the castle, she thought we might like a few partridges. In a few days when they are familiar with their new surroundings, we will set them free. There is a high chance they will be tempted to the nearby fields and the wood on the hill, in which case, their eventual fate will probably be the same as most of the pheasants reared by the estate keeper and released into the wood for shooting. Some of these pheasants have developed the habit of flying into the garden as soon as the beaters and guns appear. They seem to know it is the safest place to be; it is not unusual for us to see at least a dozen pheasants in the garden during a shoot. Two or three of those pheasants are now residents and come to be fed along with the other fowl, and even roost close to the peacocks in the same cedar tree. Hopefully the partridges will look upon the castle garden and grounds as their home. I visualise them in the summer, wandering contentedly through the orchard with the guinea fowl, foraging amongst fine grasses and wild flowers. These thoughts of summer are particularly strong just now as large flakes of thick snow fall through the inky night sky.

In the early morning sunshine, fox tracks through the garden are the only signs of disturbance on the smooth carpet of crisp, glazed snow. In the purity of the snow, the castle and garden assume an altered perspective. Where late winter's morning sun routinely casts light and shade, the layer of snow now adds a different dimension, creating new highlights and shadows. Buttresses supporting the low wall of the east border stand out boldly from the surrounding, snow-clad masonry. Dark flanks of yew hedges create contrasting walls of

blackness against a backdrop of white. Brought into sharp focus in the clarity of the snowy light, branches of trees are displayed with architectural precision as every curve and angle is enhanced.

For the past two weeks, *Eremurus himalaicus* has been anxious to push its developing bud above the surface of the soil. Planted at the shady side of the gatehouse, it must surely struggle with the damp soil and lack of warmth, but every summer this foxtail lily produces an impressive, towering spire of flowers. I know it would prefer a warmer, sunnier site, but I am reticent to move it. It seems to respond immediately to the change in day length after the winter solstice, and by the end of January, new growth is clearly visible poking up through the soil. This fearless optimism would have disastrous consequences for the foxtail lily were it not for the thick

layer of leaf mould I pile on top of it at the first warning of impending frosty weather. Against all odds, it has survived and flowered for the past five years, but the only clue to its existence this morning is a gently mounded, protective contour on the otherwise flat expanse of snow on the gatehouse border.

The first mole in recent years to inhabit the vegetable garden has been working in the early hours of the morning, casting three new black heaps of soil on top of the snow covering the grass paths.

The snow lay for most of last week, melting only slightly during the days and then freezing at nights. Now there is not a trace.

Signs of winter's demise are becoming noticeable. Along the shaded base of the gatehouse wall, small colonies of *Asplenium scolopendrium* and *Arum italicum* have already produced new foliage. The dark green leaves of *Arum* are marbled and mottled, their spear-shaped symmetry noticeable against the background of stone. They also grow amongst the grass, tucked between the stems of long-established rambling roses that tumble over the roadside wall into the sunshine displaying their fountains of blossom in summer. Ripples of pink on the soil surface beside the gatehouse signal the cautious emergence of *Dicentra formosa* while leaf tips of 'White Triumphator' tulips tentatively push up through to the light.

During the past week, we released the six French partridges, one each day, in the hope they remain in the garden. For a few days, their absence made it seem likely they had all flown away, but yesterday two reappeared in our yard. Last night they settled down together, huddled against the woodshed door in pouring rain. It caused problems for us bringing in logs for our evening fire but we did not disturb them. This morning, around seven o'clock, the two birds fed contentedly on some grain before they walked round to the vegetable garden. Of the six partridges, perhaps this pair will decide to make the garden their home.

The first daffodils of the year are always to be found in the herbaceous border beside the orchard. These daffodils are vigorous and large, and although they look out of place growing amongst the clumps of perennials, I am very fond of them. We try to use as many of them as possible as cut flowers, but they never weaken. At this time each year, I make a promise to move them to a more appropriate place where they can grow and flower in peace. The optimum time to move them would be when their foliage has just

faded but before the rampant growth of the surrounding herbaceous plants becomes too heavy and dense. But when that time comes in late May, the garden is so demanding and we are preoccupied with grass cutting, planting out and weeding. Thoughts of daffodils are then far from our minds.

Aware of the rapid development of flower buds on the daffodils, I have been working along the herbaceous border, cutting back last year's dried and brittle foliage and forking leaf mould into the soil. Even though the daffodils here are not entirely welcome, it seems churlish not to prepare for their display of blossom. Their bright and cheerful flowers will have a tidy and tended backdrop. At soil level, bright red, pointed buds of *Paeonia* are waiting like coiled springs, ready to burst into action. Because there is always a fear of accidentally standing on them during the process of clearing and mulching, I mark the position of each plant with a cane before I start. Such old, established plants deserve respect. Towards the end of the border nearest the moat, a group of *Primula auricula* are looking fresh and lively with dusty, new foliage. They were given to the bishop as a present after he admired them in a friend's garden. We know they have clear, yellow flowers, but we have no record of the variety name. I kept three plants in pots in case those planted in the border were not happy with their new abode. But it seems all is well, and it looks as if there should be a fine display of *P. auricula* flowers in the spring.

Most of the day was dedicated to the drive. Spectacular carpets of snowdrops beneath the trees were glistening in the sunlight after an early morning frost. After I raked leaves and twigs from the grass

borders along edges of the road, Jim followed behind with a mower. This idea was not to cut the grass, but instead to have a sweeping, combing effect, leaving the grass borders pristine and green while offsetting the longer grass behind. Already, tufts of dark green, glossy foliage of bluebells are beginning to become distinguishable amongst the grass. Snowdrop flowers, daffodil buds and bluebell leaves are here all at once, suddenly appearing within only two weeks.

Undoubtedly attracted to the developing buds of flowering cherries, bullfinches were darting between the branches of trees and shrubs. We rarely see them in the garden, not even in the orchard, but they regularly frequent the drive. Distant flashes of their pink and white colouring in the bright sunlight are all we see as they flutter around. Only occasionally do we catch a nearby glimpse of these shy birds.

Some of the seed I sowed in the greenhouse last month has germinated. The first sowing of sweet peas has not been so successful, but I admit it is my own fault. Not wanting to throw out sweet pea seed left over from two previous years, I decided to sow them, but there was obviously no life beneath the smooth, hard-coated surface of these perfectly round seeds. I have now sown pots of fresh seed – as many pots as I can fit onto the heated bench. Packets of seed of hardy trees and shrubs are still residing in our fridge in the butter compartment, hopefully fooling the seed into believing they are enduring a long, cold winter.

Frozen ground, in all but the most sheltered, south-facing borders, is precluding us from working with the soil. We need to finish off digging leaf mould and compost into a few remaining vegetable beds. I would also like to mulch and lightly fork over the half of the white and purple border that I optimistically planned to complete in December. Before we know it, the new season will be upon us, and there is peace of mind in knowing that all the digging and mulching has been done before the rush of spring work begins.

Instead, we spent the afternoon in the orchard. There were two reasons for this. The orchard is one of the sunniest areas of the garden, and on a cold, frosty day, there is nothing better and more reassuring than feeling the heat of February's sun through layers of winter clothes. Piles of branches resulting from pruning and reshaping the old apple trees have been accumulating since late autumn. That work is now coming to an end, and as Jim added a few final touches to the shaping of the trees, I piled the barrow high with the angular branches and took them round to the bonfire area beside the gatehouse. In theory, it is now too late to be working among the apple trees, but when running a garden, it is very difficult to adhere to all the theories.

Throughout the year, the old apple trees bring great character and charm to the garden; blossom in spring, crimson and amber fruit in late summer and autumn, and the gnarled features of winter's grey-barked nakedness telling tales but keeping decades of secrets.

Four yew trees grow against the south-facing wall of the apothecary's garden. The lower ten feet of growth is maintained as a neatly clipped hedge, but high above, the trees grow as they wish, in this case straggly and wild with no defined shape. From the garden they look strange and unsightly, obscuring most of Kite's Tower from view. Looking out from the castle, they form a dense, dark barrier, hiding an especially attractive part of the garden from the eyes of anyone standing at the windows of Kite's Tower. At the same time, they steal light from the castle yard and the bishop's kitchen windows.

As we developed the apothecary's garden over the years and it grew in formality, the unruly nature of the yews became highlighted. It became increasingly obvious that the kindest act for this area of the castle garden would be to tame the yews. This week, when the soil remained frozen, but the days were still and clear, we decided the conditions were perfect for some tree work.

Long, straight, upright branches were felled, leaving at least twelve feet of growth, reaching just above the wall of Kite's Tower garden. By counting the rings in the freshly felled, central stems, we estimated

the trees to be roughly sixty years old – only a blink in the potential life of a yew. Left to grow as they were, I think their life expectancy would have been limited, but as a well-maintained, neatly-shaped hedge, there is a high chance they will now remain an integral part of the structure of this garden. As the branches were felled, we set a fire and burned the brushwood in the centre of one of the vegetable beds while keeping aside the larger pieces for firewood. The change is dramatic. The bishop's wife came down the steps at the side of the hedge while the work was in progress to say how delighted she was with the immediate increase of light into her kitchen and the more open view. She also mentioned how the smell of burning made her worry the castle was on fire, until she realised it was the smoke from our bonfire that was seeping in through windows and beneath doors. The wood smoke permeated the castle, our cottage, and the

chauffeur's cottage, but nobody complained – in fact, the bishop's wife said she found the scent of wood smoke quite agreeable.

From the apothecary's garden, much more of the castle architecture is now visible. The eye is led across the garden to the previously obscured features of roof-top crenellations and the arched windows of Kite's Tower.

A hint of spring drifted around the garden this morning and remained all day; balmy air, blue skies, bird song, softness of light. The first few daffodils are in bloom. In our cottage, the scent of hyacinths fills every room.

One of the guinea fowl died early this morning after being chased and caught by a dog a few days ago. Hopeful that it might recover from its injuries, we kept it in a box of straw beside the fireplace in our cottage, but it had been too badly hurt. I buried the bird in the orchard where the guinea fowl spend many summer days picking their way through the fine grasses.

Drifts of smoke seemed to be wafting through the orchard, fleetingly highlighted in the rays of the early sun. It surprised me that I was unable to catch the aroma of burning in the air, but when I saw a thrush's wings brushing against the yew tree overhanging the orchard wall, I then understood the mystery of the scentless smoke. The slightest hint of a breeze or movement amongst the yew foliage was releasing clouds of pollen from thousands of barely noticeable, male flowers, each one formed from a tiny cluster of yellow stamens. A gentle tap on one of the branches is all it takes to produce a dusty haze of pollen that floats off across the garden.

The *Magnolia sinensis* from Crathes Castle in Aberdeenshire has been sitting in its pot in our yard since it arrived here last autumn. There have been at least three sites suggested for its final destination, but in the end, we decided it should be planted beside the steps leading down into the orchard. There, it will have shelter from a south-facing wall, and when it is in bloom, the flowers will be closely visible to anyone walking down the steps. Even when viewed at a distance, *Magnolia* flowers are extravagant and sumptuous, but at close range, the full extent of their luxuriant beauty can be fully appreciated.

Seed potatoes that I stored through the winter in a small pantry adjoining our cottage have developed small, pale, hopeful sprouts. Now, they lie in wooden boxes laid out on the potting shed bench, freed from darkness and uncovered from their winter layers of newspaper. Encouraged by the light, new shoots are tinged with shades of green, pink and purple. They will slowly develop – a process known as chitting. There are twenty-two varieties to plant this year, and much though I would like to keep collecting more, I am limited by space.

A beech hedge, overgrown and tangled with hawthorn, running the whole length of the garden, parallel to the footpath leading down to Rose Bridge, is always an awkward area for us to maintain. Jim has been working his away along it for the past few years, reducing the height and reshaping it. One more section remains, awaiting attention. For a few hours this afternoon, three of us set about the hedge. As Jim reduced the height with the chainsaw, the young man who helps us in the garden pulled the tangled mass of cut stems free while I tended the bonfire at the side of the footpath where the branches were soon reduced to ash. Clearing up afterwards had to be scrupulous – cattle use this path to walk to and from their pasture from the milking parlour at the farm, and thorns cause trouble if they become lodged in their hooves.

MARCH

Tight domes of crumpled, pink and red foliage are beginning to look out above the surface of the rhubarb bed. As Jim continued shaping the yew hedge in the apothecary's garden, I forked over the soil between the solid rhubarb crowns and added a generous amount of leaf mould at the same time. When we looked at photographs last night that I had taken of 'before and after' work on the yew hedge, we decided it should be lowered even further to the match the height of the wall of Kite's Tower. Last week, we had suspected that wall-level would be its natural, finished height, but rather than regret cutting it back too far, we left the hedge a few feet taller to let our eyes become accustomed to it for a few days. Unfortunately, the roof of a small wooden shed in Kite's Tower garden is now in full view behind the hedge and wall, but we will move the shed in the near future – we have quiet plans for its redeployment as a henhouse.

In the soft fruit area, beside the rhubarb bed, there are three long, narrow beds of raspberry canes. 'Glen Moy', 'Glen Clova' and 'Autumn Bliss' provide a small but reliable crop of berries from midsummer until autumn. 'Autumn Bliss' bears the largest quantity of fruit, but that is because its production of fruit in late summer is less attractive to birds than fruit of the other varieties borne earlier in the season. A large fruit cage would be ideal, but at the moment most of the raspberries are shared with the birds. This afternoon, I cut all the 'Autumn Bliss' canes to ground level and then mulched the soil. My supply of leaf mould for this year is coming to an end so I am being selective about which beds or plants are receiving the last few precious barrow loads.

A whole month has passed since we brought the six French partridges to Rose Castle. Two birds, hopefully a breeding pair, are now settled in the garden, seeming content to spend their days lingering in the dusty, dry environs along the edges of beech and yew hedges, and always choosing the sunny side. Without fail, they come to our yard to be fed in the evenings, first surveying the scene for about ten minutes from the potting shed roof, before flying down to the gravel.

On a routine, early morning wander through the greenhouse, I noticed three seeds of *Colutea arborescens* had germinated. From interest, and because I have never grown it before, I have also sown seed of *Colutea x media*, the red flowering species. If any germinate and grow on successfully, I will find a sheltered, sunny site for this new introduction to Rose.

Just when we thought one pair of French partridges was established in the garden, it was sad to see only one of the birds waiting patiently on the potting shed roof for its evening food. For the past few days, only a single partridge has been seen. I fear this garden is not a safe environment for partridges roosting on the ground at night, especially when there is only one pair. Reading up on the subject, I have discovered that they are safer in large numbers when there are more pairs of eyes at night to keep a watch for foxes and cats.

It has been one of the best years for spring bulbs. They are all growing with such enthusiasm and vigour. Even the delicate *Crocus chrysanthus* 'Blue Pearl' and 'Cream Beauty', which in previous years barely managed to produce their small silken flowers, have borne a flush of healthy strong blooms. This year, for the first time, their flowers are prolific, opening in the afternoon sunlight to reveal the full beauty of their subtle colouring. I find them so much more pleasing to the eye than the large-flowered hybrids.

The carpet of grass beneath the trees in the drive is beginning to develop the fresh, green sheen of spring. At the same time, snowdrops, daffodils and a few purple crocus are blooming together, while tufts of dark, glossy, bluebell foliage are gaining height daily. I do not recall a year when the flowering times of snowdrops and daffodils have been so close together.

About six years ago, Jim planted small groups of *Leucojum vernum* in the grass by the entrance gates to the castle drive. At the moment, they are in full bloom, providing an attractive display, not only for visitors to the castle, but for passers-by or people who stop to post their letters at the post box beside the sandstone pillars. The original plants came from the small enclosed walled area at the bottom of the orchard where large numbers of them flower each year. It seemed better to move them to a place where they could be fully admired and appreciated.

Watering young plants in the glasshouse, feeding the peacocks and guinea fowl, and letting the geese out of their shed are my early morning, routine jobs. Usually I never see another person at this time of day, apart from distant views of the farmer tending his cattle

after milking. This morning, however, I was greeted by the bishop, dressed in his liturgical purple shirt and enjoying the morning air, no doubt in advance of a busy schedule where he would see little more of the day's natural sunlight. His main interest this morning was the whereabouts of the partridges as he had yet to see them at close quarters. Fortunately, his timing was perfect; the remaining partridge was sitting on top of the potting shed roof, unconcerned about being viewed so closely.

Cold nights are followed by frosty mornings with clear blue skies. The warmth of the sun has been coaxing flower buds on apple and cherry trees to reveal the first glimpse of colour. *Prunus x yedoensis* is showing hints of pink with a promise of blossom in only a few days. As soon as I walk through the cottage door into the yard, I see the silhouettes of flowers on poplar trees becoming more and more pronounced against the backdrop of the northern sky. The four poplars growing close to our cottage are situated along the bank of the bog garden. This morning, I thought I caught just a hint of the sweet scent of poplar foliage. As garden trees, poplars are often criticised, but I like them purely for the mellifluous fragrance that fills the air on warm spring days. So often, visitors to Gardener's Cottage at this time of year have been spellbound by the honey-scented air, not realising they were standing only a few yards from the source, high up above them in the poplars.

The dark green foliage of *Fritillaria meleagris*, better known as snake's head lily, is rising above the height of the grass. Small flower buds are curled beneath protective stems. Although we have planted many over the years, most of the snake's head lilies grow on a narrow, grassy bank that separates the herbaceous border from the orchard. Every year, they increase in number, but our only problem is that guinea fowl find them irresistible and tend to treat the flowers as a great delicacy. It was a couple of years before I managed to discover the reason for flowers that were missing or tattered and torn when, one April morning, I came across the guinea fowl contentedly working their way along the bank, enjoying a feast of the papery, snakeskin petals.

This afternoon's sun was warm enough for me to shed winter layers and work with bare arms in the gatehouse border. Tulip leaves are moving through the moist soil, reaching up towards the new season, and any work in this bed has to be gentle and precise to save damaging the developing flowers.

Later in the afternoon, I noticed the bishop's wife walking through the garden with a friend. They lingered along the path through the newly planted woodland in the field to the west of the castle, bending to look closely at young trees. The small Scots pine are particularly healthy and exuberant; their new, symmetrical branches, topped with tufts of green needles have the appearance of candelabras.

The dullness and creeping dampness of last spring seem far away now as we soak up heat of the sun. It is a day for lingering and spending a few moments just to wonder at the beauty of nature. The bishop's chaplain often walks round the garden on his lunch hour; it is, he says, one of the best ways to clear his mind. Today as he stopped to speak while as I was tidying the delphinium beds, he was also obviously enjoying the peacefulness and warmth of this spring day.

Wednesday is fish day at the castle. The fishman takes great interest in the number of birds and red squirrels he sees as he makes his way up the drive in his refrigerated van. Choosing and buying the fish is always a bit of an early morning, social event, with the bishop's chauffeur and sometimes the bishop himself, coming into the van. Squirrels are often the first topic of conversation, then there is usually much laughter and joviality with the fishman's happy-go-lucky outlook on life and sense of humour transmitted to us all before he sets off to the square in the village.

Aubretia is flowing down the sunny side of the gatehouse walls. They are growing there by chance, the result of seeds blown into cracks in the ancient masonry. Looking from the castle through the

arch of the gatehouse, the eye is drawn to cascades of purple flowers. A few of last year's self-sown seedlings are thriving at the base of the wall, but they have an uncertain future there. With a trowel, I eased the healthiest of these tiny plants from the soil and brought them round to our cottage. They are now safely ensconced between cracks and crevices in the paving at the bottom of the steps leading down from our back door. Perhaps next spring we will have pools of purple spreading across red sandstone slabs.

The joiners arrived to replace the west gates to the vegetable garden. The old, wooden gates have become more and more battered during the past few years; time and high winds have taken their toll, with their final demise during a night of gales last November. When we first arrived here, these gates remained firmly closed at all times, but as work progressed on the vegetable garden, and it was transformed from one rectangular expanse of bare soil into an area of small beds with grass paths between, we started to leave the gates open day and night. Walkers passing on the footpath that runs along the outside of the west wall then had a clear view into the vegetable garden; it seemed better that people who were interested or curious would be able to admire the garden without having to peer uncomfortably over the top of the high wall. Lately, the old, battered gates had imparted a world-weary appearance. Some time in the future, we may get a set of ornate, heavy, black metal gates for the vegetable garden, matching the general style of the small garden gates.

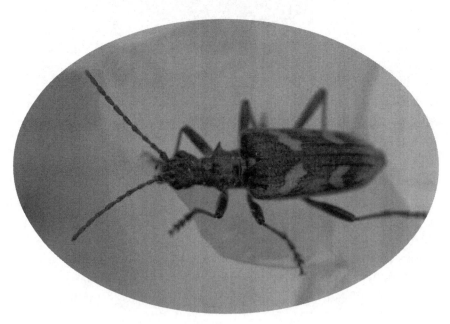

Lettuce sown last month in the glasshouse is now planted out in a covered frame. Before long, there will be a selection of fresh, young leaves for salads. The frame sits on one of the vegetable beds and is the only method we have of raising an early crop of low-growing vegetables. Three weeks ago, I sowed some rocket in the glasshouse to see if it could be forced into growth earlier than usual without becoming too stretched and leggy. It is now also planted in the fame beside the lettuce. Normally, I would sow it straight into the open ground in May and harvest the young leaves in June. Because the small beds in the vegetable garden have been laid out in a symmetrical fashion, the large wooden frame sitting on one bed upsets the balance, especially at this time of year when the layout of the bare, brown beds is crisp and clear with no foliage to blend the outlines. This spring, Jim is planning to make another frame to match the existing one, therefore re-establishing the symmetry of the garden and providing more space for growing early salad crops.

Mists and dusty frosts clear away to reveal sparkling spring mornings. Surely this month of March must have been one of the driest and sunniest on record. *Forsythia* and *Prunus x yedoensis* are in full bloom and the display of daffodils in the drive is at its peak. The first snake's head lilies are now revealing their pendulous flowers, bell-shaped and reptilian in appearance. One wonders why evolution destined them to have such mysterious flowers. Planted in groups, these *Fritillaria meleagris* always attract attention; their snake's skin flowers hanging so delicately from slender stems.

I planted the first of twenty-two varieties of potatoes today; 'Pentland Javelin', 'Nicola', 'Ratte' and 'Belle de Fontenay'. As soon as December turns to January, I eagerly await this special day of spring when potatoes, fully chitted, are taken from their wooden boxes in the potting shed, dropped into crumbly soil, covered over, and urged into growth by moist darkness and lengthening days.

APRIL

April blew in, stormy and wet. Torrential rain was like a fountain caught in the wind with swirling spray all around. Usually orderly in their morning flight, rooks were now tatters of blackness, blown indiscriminately like fragments of ragged silk across the grey skies. Daffodils that had grown tall and soft in the calmness of March's sunshine and warm days were dishevelled and broken. The day displayed April's true characteristics; hail, blustery showers, sunshine and cloud, all in equal quantities. In today's newspaper they noted that this year's March had been the sunniest and warmest recorded since 1907.

Although the days are noticeably more chilly and blustery, I continued planting potatoes. Small tubers, many no bigger than marbles, of 'Salad Blue', 'Shetland Black' and 'Highland Burgundy

Red' were given pride of place in beds with the best soil. This will be their first year planted out in the garden, having been raised in pots last year from tiny micro-propagated plants that were posted to me from a specialist potato company. I knew of these varieties, but was never able to obtain any until I went to the Potato Day at Galashiels last March. For those who are fascinated by potatoes, this annual event is an essential date in the calendar. Hundreds of varieties of seed potatoes are displayed for sale, and experts are available to answer questions and discuss every possible nuance concerning potatoes. I was interested last year to see some freeze-dried potato from South America, known as chuno – a staple diet amongst people living there in remote areas.

Every year, I notice an improvement in the soil in the vegetable beds. The copious, winter supply of leaf mould, farm yard manure, compost, scrapings from the bottom of the old goose shed, and anything else I can find, is slowly breaking down the heavy soil. Potatoes respond to the soil's open texture, but in beds with soil that needs more attention and winter work, the potatoes tend to become infested with slugs at an early date. Variety names are clearly marked on large labels, easy to read without bending down. Visitors to the garden like to know the names, with most people never having seen so many varieties grown in such a relatively small area. Rotation is important, but I have to look at last year's photographs of the garden to ensure that the potatoes are planted in fresh soil.

Carpets of wood anemones have colonised large areas beneath the beech trees in the drive. Throughout the night, their petals are neatly folded and protective, but by mid-morning, their creamy white flowers are fully open as they bask in the spring sunshine. Most of them are established in mossy areas where there is little competition from strongly growing grasses. They have always been here in small numbers, but this spring they have appeared in great abundance, like shining pools of white light on the woodland floor. The previous bishop was so fond of these anemones, he would stop his car on the drive, even if on his way to an important event, and walk over to have a close look at the flowers.

Mature damson and greengage trees in the orchard are covered in clouds of white blossom, eagerly attended by small bumble bees that move ceaselessly amongst the sunlit flowers. Younger trees, planted about four years ago to ensure a traditional continuation of the orchard in the event of the loss of the older trees, are also clad with fresh, white blossom. Lush grass forms a flowing, green velvet carpet on the orchard floor with finely cut paths snaking smoothly between the trees. At this time of year, it is the most beautiful part of the garden.

There are three of Jim's hand-made, wooden seats to choose from in the orchard, each one positioned to catch the sun at different times of the day. Secluded by rhododendrons, but open to the fullness of the afternoon sun, a bench at the end of the orchard nestles beneath a cherry tree with branches pendulous and heavy with blossom. This must be the finest April afternoon seat, especially when white petals float gently down like the first flakes of winter snow to settle on the wooden table beside my coffee cup. A group of daffodils, 'Professor Einstein', are planted in this secret area, their white and orange flowers in full bloom beneath the canopy of cherry blossom.

The vegetable garden is assuming an air of orderliness and expectation. In the beds where the potatoes are planted, there are small but prominent ridges of soil, neatly arranged in rows like miniature mountain ranges. Rows of parsley that were planted in midsummer are now the most vivid shade of green. Spinach, too, is producing bright, new, tender leaves and fills three of the smaller beds with its conspicuous foliage. Sorrel, probably not used much in the castle kitchen but a favourite of mine for adding a hint of sharpness to salads, forms a neat, low row of greenery. In one of the beds closest to the grass paths, chives are already ten inches tall. Their young, self-sown seedlings from last year are growing like a carpet of grass in neighbouring beds, but are only a minor irritation; a quick fork through the soil on a sunny afternoon and they are

soon disestablished. Some gardeners remove the flowers of chives to prevent this problem, but I am too fond of these rounded clusters of blossom that bring shades of dark lilac to the garden in early summer. Less easily controlled are the seedlings of angelica. Even the youngest plants have long, tenacious roots. Jim's idea was to have two angelica plants in the beds either side of the round central bed. Their imperious height imparts stateliness and drama, but the resulting seedlings are an annoyance. Not only are they to be found in neighbouring beds, but they also arise in the most unpredictable areas of the garden where they are not always welcome. Once again, their seed heads should be removed to prevent this problem, but I can never bring myself to remove these statuesque globes. Although it brings its problems, angelica is still an integral part of the vegetable garden, and I can stand next to a plant, taller than myself, that has attained this height and shape in only a few weeks.

There can be few greater contrasts to the rural, tranquillity of Rose Castle garden than the hustle and bustle of a Mediterranean city. A few days spent in the old part of Barcelona last week was enlightening and energising. Jim and I had time to wander through the maze of narrow, cobbled streets that every so often opened out onto paved plazas planted with *Washingtonia* palms or groups of *Albizia*. Large, papery *Albizia* seeds were blowing around in the streets by the harbour so I collected a few to bring back to Rose Castle to sow. Market stalls overflowed with fruit, vegetables and fresh fish. Crimson strawberries were arranged in tall, elaborate pyramids. On our train journeys to and from the city, we passed between fields of artichokes and broad beans already in flower. I thought of our broad beans at Rose Castle, only just appearing above the surface of the compost in the protected environment of the glasshouse.

While we were away, our friend from Raughtonhead who was the drummer in our small band for the bishop's birthday party last August looked after the glasshouses and cold frames. Sunny days had followed frosty nights and he kindly took the trouble to move young plants from the frames back into the glasshouses.

On our return to Rose Castle, cutting as much grass as possible was the main objective and fortunately it remained dry and windy all day. The bishop was spending some time late this afternoon looking round the garden and grounds, returning to the castle to collect his camera after seeing our three newly hatched goslings sitting amongst the buttercups, closely guarded by the goose and gander.

Still the warmth and sunshine continues – so warm it feels unnatural, but certainly not unwelcome. Jim concentrated on cutting grass and manicuring the drive, carefully leaving swathes of grass uncut where primroses and wood anemones are flowering and where the foliage of bluebells, red campion and ragged robin is visible. Meanwhile, in the vegetable garden, I planted onion sets in the open ground and sowed more rocket beneath cloches. The miniature cauliflower, 'Clarke', were large enough to be transplanted into the covered frame where they are protected from the chilly night air and the peacocks' appetite for all young plants related to the cabbage family. Although the peacocks are trained to stay out of the vegetable garden in spring, they occasionally carry out early morning raids. Grown for the first time last year, the cauliflower were a great success and much admired by the bishop's wife. Because they are an early variety, they miss the damaging feeding frenzies of the cabbage white butterfly caterpillars that attack all our brassica crops with great abandon later in the summer. 'Clarke' forms neat little heads of pure white florets, and although the wide, leafy foliage takes up much space in proportion to the size of the usable vegetable, it is still an appealing crop to grow. As soon as they are all harvested, I can sow more lettuce or rocket in their place.

This evening, we decided to make the most of this wave of warm, balmy air by dining 'al fresco'. Surrounded by bird song and watching the sun sink below the trees to the west of the castle, we

had just finished eating when we noticed the bishop walking through the vegetable garden. Since we removed the fences three or four years ago, Gardener's Cottage garden now merges into the main grass path of the vegetable garden, and when the bishop saw us sat in the evening light, he wandered down towards us past the pear trees thickly covered in white blossom. He too, was captivated with the peacefulness and warmth of the evening and sat down to chat for a while. Jim opened a bottle of red wine as the conversation flowed around our recent visit to Barcelona and the bishop's own experience of Spain. Before he made his way round to the front of the castle where he was expecting guests, we walked back through the garden. He referred to previous notes in his garden notebook when inquiring about plants in the herbaceous border and trees in the woodland, trying all the time to increase his knowledge of botanical names. He did point out with good-natured exasperation that it is not always easy for him to learn the names of perennials by referring to his notes because I am in the habit of moving plants around from place to place. Looking down from the white and purple border towards the moat, he was particularly intrigued by the different shapes and forms of birch, all of which are *Betula pendula* but with contrasting characteristics due to varying provenance of seed. Their leafless silhouettes and pale stems stood out in the low, evening light.

On Easter Sunday the first pair of swallows to return to Rose Castle announced their arrival with darting, swooping flights and incessant chatter. Within hours, they were already flitting in and out of open sheds and garages, checking for potential nesting sites. The promise of summer glanced from their sharp wings.

Today, white petals from damson flowers float down from the trees. Pink and white apple blossom unfurls along old, bumpy, grey branches and also clothes the smoother, upright stems of younger trees. The past few weeks of warmth have encouraged herbaceous plants to produce early, long, soft growth with the result that the perennial borders are already assuming a summer appearance with large, rounded mounds of foliage in dark, dusty or silvery shades of green.

'Handel', a climbing rose growing against the south-facing wall of Gardener's Cottage, is showing just a sliver of pink petals from buds that are enticed by sunshine-filled days. This rose was a favourite of Lady Aberdeen's from her childhood in the south of England, but even the most sheltered wall at Haddo House could never offer it

the required degree of protection from cold, Aberdeenshire winds. In my nine years as head gardener there, I can remember planting at least three specimens of this rose in an attempt to coax just one or two flowers. At Rose Castle, 'Handel' flowers well in the softer Cumbrian climate, but its lack of robustness ensures I treat it with great care. As every delicate, pink and white flower opens, I am reminded of Lady Aberdeen and our long struggle and endless wish for 'Handel' to flower at Haddo.

Now that the soil has absorbed so much warmth from weeks of sunshine, high humidity and April showers have provoked a rapid surge of growth throughout the garden.

The glasshouses and cold frames are full of young plants and I am sure I could manage to utilise even more space. I expect all gardeners have the same problem. This morning, I noticed signs of germination from one of the *Pinus coulteri* seeds I sowed in February – a strong, pale green, curved shoot about to rise from its pot of compost. Of the other tree seeds I sowed, *Picea breweriana* has had the best germination rate; there are now at least one dozen small trees, no more than one inch high, waiting to be transplanted into single pots. I envisage a grove of these graceful trees with their pendulous branches hanging like long, combed hair: a Rose Castle, hanging garden of weeping spruce.

In the covered raised bed, the first crop of lettuce and rocket is ready for use. A new batch of young lettuce plants is now ready for

planting. Every month I will sow more to ensure a succession of fresh, crisp lettuce throughout summer and most of autumn. At the moment, they are being sown in individual pots in the greenhouse, but by the end of May when the risk of frost has passed, I will be able to sow them straight into the soil in the raised beds. Rocket seed that I sowed beneath a cloche has now germinated and the rows of young plants will have to be thinned as soon as possible.

This morning, as I walked through the garden on my way back from collecting the newspapers from the box at the end of the drive, I noticed *Geranium phaeum* in full bloom in the herbaceous border. There are several plants in flower, each with blossom in varying degrees of purple, some very dark indeed. In the tiny garden dedicated to Bishop Nicolson who left behind Rose Castle plant lists from the 1700s, bright blue flowers of *Anchusa azurea* shine out from the shady backdrop of a nearby yew tree that stands not far from the rustic table and seat made by Jim from the wood of the huge, mature cedar that fell in the Boxing Day gale. Just around the corner, in deeper shade close to the wall, white flowers of wild garlic are starry and bright. Each year, wild garlic works its way further along the base of the north wall beside the grass path at the top of the woodland bank, but as it is not unattractive, and much more preferable than ground elder, we leave it to wander freely. If it were to colonise the whole length of the wall, it would be a pleasant feature at this time of year.

Birds are nesting everywhere: beneath the lean-to shed in our yard, in the cypress hedge separating the gardens of the two cottages, in a bird box in the chauffeur's garden, beneath the slates of our coal house, and even in the old post box in the castle yard. During the warm weeks earlier this month, I left the greenhouse door open all day, but unbeknown to me at the time, a blackbird came in to build a nest of dried grass, garden twine, goose down and guinea fowl feathers amongst the tangle of passionflower stems tied to the whitewashed wall. I found the nest a few days ago, but the bird had obviously decided by then to relocate elsewhere when it realised the greenhouse door is not always left open.

MAY

Last year's 'Red Gauntlet' strawberry plants are bearing copious trusses of white flowers, fully visible only when you bend down and move aside the foliage. Most of the afternoon was spent removing healthy colonies of buttercups that were trying to encroach and compete for space. At the same time, I dug in last year's thick layer of straw, forking it into the soil between the plants. The heavy soil should benefit from this addition of fibrous, organic material, but having said that, the strawberries have thrived in their slightly less than optimum conditions. The bed is now ready for a layer of fresh straw. If May is a month with no frost, the flowers will be free to continue their development into a summer crop of sweet, juicy berries.

The resident red squirrel, so tame that it comes to the cottages each morning and evening to be fed, put on an impressive and unforgettable display today. In the past, we have seen it run up the whole length of a smooth, painted drainpipe; in fact, if we are not careful, it uses this method to come into our cottage in the summer via an open upstairs window. This morning, however, it ran straight up the rough sandstone surface of the castle wall, all the way to the top of Kite's Tower, where it then proceeded to run around in a frenzied, carefree and daring fashion, jumping across crenellations, balancing precariously on narrow ledges, leaping and twisting through the air. We were standing in the yard, looking up to the castle roof to watch this spectacle, when the squirrel misjudged a distance and fell from the very top of Kite's Tower, landing on the tarmac not far away from us. The bishop, who happened to be in the kitchen at the time was becoming curious; he could he see a gathering of people in the yard looking upwards, and then he saw something fall past the kitchen window. When he came out to see what was happening, the motionless squirrel was lying close to the back door. To the amazement of us all, it rolled over, gave itself a shake, and ran off towards the cedar trees. It returned in the evening to the back door of the chauffeur's cottage to be fed, seemingly none the worse for its dramatic tumble from the top of Rose Castle.

Frenetic grass cutting, edging, hoeing and weeding during the past few days was in preparation for a visit to Rose Castle today by employees of the Church Commissioners from other parts of the country. Many had never been here before, and of those who had, most had no idea of the extent and content of the gardens. Jim and I led a walk through the garden that was followed by a guided tour through the castle by the bishop's wife and the chauffeur. Fortunately the sun broke out from behind grey clouds to display the orchard in its full beauty. As the

visitors walked along closely cut, grass paths between trees clad in pink
blossom, they marvelled at the quietness and tranquillity. Throughout
the orchard, long grasses swayed in the breeze as swallows skimmed
over the tops of the tallest flower heads. After lunch in the castle
dining room, those who were keen to learn more about the garden
walked round again at their leisure. We showed this smaller group the
behind-the-scenes areas: cold frames, glasshouses, machinery and
potting shed – often the most interesting parts of a garden to serious
gardeners. The potting shed always draws wistful looks and sighs of
admiration. Wooden shelves on cobwebbed walls are stacked with
dusty clay pots belonging to another era. The tell-tale signs of our
winter fires in the shed were highly visible: freshly layered soot above
the fireplace, wood ash in the grate, and an old-fashioned, red, metal
bucket filled with sand and the word 'fire' painted on its side.

A visit to Drummond Castle Gardens in Perthshire this afternoon left me in no doubt that the moat at Rose Castle would be a perfect canvas for formality, especially as intricate, detailed patterns of planting could be viewed from the terrace above. Few properties have such an ideal open space and perfect backdrop. I imagine walking through the orchard with its long grasses, wild flowers and apple blossom, and then, within seconds, looking down upon a dramatic, contrasting, symmetrical layout of Italianate style.

Rusty, red foliage of *Euphorbia griffithii* 'Fireglow' has a strange effect on the eye in the early morning light. It grows in profusion in the gatehouse border, and at times, its coppery hues seem to clash with the soft pink tones of the sandstone walls. At a time of year when *Euphorbia* is most colourful, one hundred 'White Triumphator' tulips are also in full bloom, the glistening whiteness of their pointed petals shining out from the gatehouse border. Pots of tomato 'Ailsa Craig' are set out for the summer in the cool greenhouse. Dahlias are still taking up space there, but they will be moved to the cold frame at the end of this week. After the unusually warm weather we had in early spring, the nights are now chilly and ground frost is still forecast.

The white and purple border is growing whiter by the day. Compact mounds of white *Viola cornuta* are in full bloom along the edge of the border, while clumps of *Hesperis matronalis*, with newly opened flowers in shades of purple, lilac and white, are tall and willowy towards the back of the border. Woolly foliage of *Helichrysum* and *Stachys byzantina* is creating a low, silver sheen that covers the darkness of the soil. Fresh young spires of blue lupin flowers are almost dark enough to be called purple - in most lights they look more purple than blue.

The chauffeur told us he spotted a hare at six o'clock this morning sitting beside the sweet pea trellis. We are used to seeing it in the drive, but not in the garden. We have to hope it is just a fleeting visit.

I met the bishop this morning just as he was locking the back door of the castle. He is always interested in the three young peafowl and asked if we had noticed that one of the peahens looked as if she might be nesting at the edge of the wood on the hill above the castle. As we were talking, the peahen appeared in the distance, her white breast feathers noticeable in the distant, dark shade of the trees as she walked along the fence-line of the wood.

Two summers ago, the chauffeur was woken in the early hours of the morning by a commotion in the orchard. He ran out into the garden dressed in his pyjamas and wellies to find a fresh pile of feathers: the fox had killed the peahen that had been roosting with her chicks on the lowest limb of the damson tree. At that time, she was our only peahen, brought here by the previous bishop's wife. The chauffeur reached the orchard in time to see the peahen's five two-week-old chicks scattering in all directions. After listening for their faint chirping, he managed to find them all amongst the long grass and beneath the yew hedges. Three chicks survived the trauma and we managed to rear them in our yard just outside the potting shed. It was never our intention to have more than one pair of peafowl in the castle grounds but it seemed cruel to separate or abandon the three young chicks to a new home, so they have remained here ever since along with the original, old peacock. The old peacock is biddable and well trained, knowing he must stay away from the vegetable garden in spring and summer, but it has to be said that 'the three chicks', as they are still known, can cause a few problems. They are now, however, very much part of the castle, and their raids on the vegetable garden seem to be less frequent.

Last night we gave a talk to a local society about Rose Castle garden. Jim concentrated on the historical aspects of the garden and I added detailed information on plants. The collection of photographs that I have taken during the past eight years helped to illustrate the talk, and later in the evening I played some fiddle tunes with Jim accompanying me on the bodhran. It is always interesting to note the points that raise the most questions; in this case potatoes and compost heaps were the most discussed topics. A photograph of our

leaf mould amphitheatre seemed to capture the imagination and was the stimulus for much discussion at the end of the night.

Damp soil and humid air is perfect just now for planting out young annuals. The weather forecast is adamant that we have seen the last frost and can look forward to warmer days next week. Just in case cold winds arise, I restricted my planting to the sheltered beds beside the gatehouse. Bright pink *Cosmos*, with the appropriate name of 'Dazzler', and purple statice, *Limonium sinuatum* 'Purple Attraction', should create a long-lasting summer display. Delicate, pink, papery flowers of *Acroclinium* planted around the edges of the beds will catch the eye of visitors as they walk through the arch.

On one side of the archway, flower spikes of *Verbascum hybrida* 'Snow Maiden' are beginning to erupt from rosettes of woolly foliage. Grown as a biennial, this plant spends its first summer subdued and anonymous, never giving away a hint of the impact it is going to make the following year. Rather than make a habit of planting annuals at either side of the gatehouse, I decided to use one of the beds for plants with an element of surprise and unexpected habit. Throughout last summer and this year's spring, 'Snow Maiden' foliage formed pleasing ground cover, but the present rate of energetic growth of the robust flower spikes is an outstanding characteristic at the moment.

As I spread straw around the strawberry plants, I was thinking of the sweet, dark red berries that would be ready for picking in a few weeks. White flowers, supported by their collars of crisp, dry straw are now safe from damaging late frosts that can turn their yellow centres black overnight. For the past two years, only one bed in the apothecary's garden has been used for growing strawberries, but the fruit has been

so popular and has grown so well that we decided last summer to plant up another full bed with runners from the parent plants. The farmer supplies us with small, rectangular bales of straw that are a handy size for working with in the garden. Any left over straw is kept for winter bedding for the goose shed. When I now look at the apothecary's garden with two beds of strawberry plants established at the top end, the idea of planting two more beds becomes tempting. Four beds would complete a symmetrical planting, and there would be even more strawberries for all to enjoy at Rose Castle.

The new mower that was delivered in early spring means we have wider scope for keeping more areas of grass under control. Instead of leaving the moat to grow wild, Jim is now keeping most of it cut. In February and March, the farmer puts sheep into the moat to graze

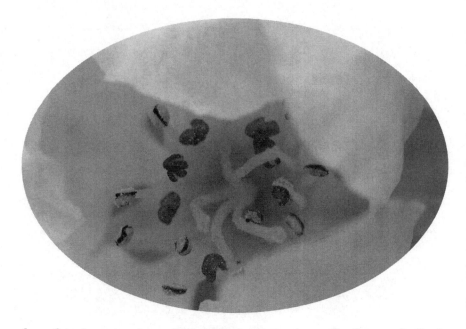

for a few days at a time which helps to keep down the first, early flush of grass. Although the wide sweep of long grass in midsummer has much charm and attracts lots of wildlife, the cut grass tends to form a better visual foreground for the walls and buttresses. We will leave one long bank of grass uncut so that there is still a habitat for the insects and goldfinches.

Everything requires staking, all at once. Tomatoes in the greenhouse, broad beans in the vegetable garden, lilies in front of the bishop's offices, and delphiniums in the borders. Bamboo canes, green twine and scissors are never far from reach just now.

The first few peas have broken through the surface of the soil in the apothecary's garden but silvery trails along the whole row show they are delectable pickings for slugs. 'Hurst Green Shaft' is the old, reliable variety I grow, and later this week I will sow another two rows for successive crops.

In the early morning, protective, pale green sheaths drop from flower buds of *Meconopsis betonicifolia* to reveal crinkled, blue petals. By midday, the flowers are fully open. This oceanic shade of blue looks so pure against a backdrop of rosy-red sandstone.

The first few flowers of *Philadelphus* opened this morning. Usually it is the first or second week in June before blossom appears. There are five established specimens of this shrub, all planted close to Gardener's Cottage. They originated from cuttings of a plant that grew in the mixed border at Haddo House garden in Aberdeenshire. I have planted them in corners and close to walls to try to capture the scent. For some people, the aroma of mock orange is too sweet and strong, but if I could, I would plant it all around my windows and doors, in the hope of enticing the fragrance to waft throughout the house. At the moment, two are planted in the cottage yard, two beside the glasshouse, and one directly beneath the bedroom window of our cottage. Last year, I took cuttings of an equally finely scented, but larger flowered, variety that grows in the chauffeur's garden. They are now growing contentedly in pots in the cold frame and will, in time, find their way into other parts of the castle garden.

Pots of lily-of-the-valley, *Convallaria majalis,* are in full flower and bring a delicate fragrance to the yard - such a sweet scent from such tiny flowers, especially in the evenings. Small pink flowers of *Convallaria* var. *rosea* are even more discreet in appearance. The original plants that I had of this particular variety came from a garden in Edinburgh and are safely planted in my mother's garden in Perthshire.

A haze of fragrance hangs above waves of white and lilac flowers of *Hesperis matronalis*. Grown in abundance, sweet rocket is so effective – I soon realised there is no point in growing only small quantities of it. At the moment, there is a *Hesperis* sea in the white and purple border – a celebration for the end of May.

JUNE

The early morning garden is tall and still, humid and hazy. Long grasses hold droplets of dew and spires of lupins are dusted with a misted filigree of spiders' webs. Languid peahens wander lazily through meadow buttercups and cow parsley in the woodland. Throughout the day, thunder rumbles in the distance. Rain clouds circle the castle from time to time, filling the air with a heady dampness before moving off to other areas.

Rain would indeed be welcome now. Seeds sown two weeks ago would benefit from a whole night of gentle rain. Spinach, chard, lettuce, rocket and coriander are waiting to break through the surface of the soil. This soil, lying so dark and heavy in the winter months, turns to the palest shade of grey whenever there is a period of dryness lasting more than a couple of weeks. Many of the annuals

planted out last week flop in the heat of the afternoon even though the sun remains behind a layer of high cloud.

Courgettes and sunflowers are last to be planted out in the vegetable garden. Although warm days in May tempted me to plant them much earlier, I know that only one night of unexpected cold winds can cause a state of shock from which it takes these plants a long time to recover. I always wait until the first week of June. Sunflowers, rarely taken seriously, bring a light-hearted, carefree touch to the garden. Every year, we plant them in three of the four corner beds of the vegetable garden. 'Italian White' is our favourite variety with its dark-centred, cream-coloured flowers that grow from branching stems. This year, for a change, we are also including groups of 'Autumn Beauty' and 'Russian Giant', planted in separate beds. Now that this habit of planting sunflowers is established, one or two self-sown seedlings appear of their own accord every summer in unexpected places, springing up from seed most probably spread by mice or birds. For the past two weeks, a rogue seedling has been growing amongst the 'Nicola' potatoes. Born into the open air, it is strong and sturdy, unlike my newly planted, greenhouse-grown plants with spindly stems already requiring canes for support.

When I walk along the orchard paths, I reach out my arms and let the palms of my hands sweep across the seed heads of waist-high timothy grass. Yellow flowers of meadow buttercups are spangled between the fine stems of the grasses, finding enough light and space to flourish. The meadow effect in the orchard has been left for as long as possible but blustery winds and showers of rain are now beginning to bend and flatten patches of the long grass, spoiling the vision. It is time for it to be cut. Jim made a start this afternoon with the rotary mower, followed by a pair of fluttering and flitting goldfinches attracted by ripe seeds shaken loose from the grasses and wild flowers. We are expecting a garden visit from about thirty people in the middle of the month and hope the orchard grass will have lost its newly cut, dishevelled appearance by that time.

Along the wall of the white and purple border, the first few blooms of *Rosa* 'Madame Alfred Carrière' have opened to reveal their white petals. Climbing roses, benefiting from shelter, are the first roses to bloom in the castle garden.

Most of the blue lavender grows in raised beds or at the base of castle's south-facing walls, but there are three plants of a white-flowered variety situated in gritty soil in a sunny bed edged with stone at the back door of Gardener's Cottage. I pick a few small bunches to hang upside down to dry.

A full day's rain yesterday enticed seedlings through the soil. Coriander and a late sowing of broad beans have finally appeared and are making rapid growth in response to their moist, warm surroundings. Star-shaped flowers in shades of cream, blue and lilac are becoming noticeable on the potatoes. At the same time, flower buds of *Rosa gallica* var. *officinalis* are showing their first glimpses of pink petals. In the apothecary's garden, thirty of these roses planted in the shape of a cross will be in full bloom within the next fortnight.

Straight, sharp outlines of newly cut hedges contrast with towering spires of delphiniums and teasels in informal areas. Where beds are symmetrical and formal, the background silhouette of green

blocks of hedging, now bereft of their loose, early, straggly growth, adds to the general orderliness. Yew hedges have yet to be trimmed, but summer's first shaping of beech and cypress hedges was finished today. Cutting a beech hedge fills the air with a sweet scent reminiscent of lime blossom; a scent that lingers throughout the garden all day leaving traces on my skin and clothes, still discernable in the evening. The sap from cypress foliage exudes strong, heady, citrus aromas, but I find it causes my skin to blister on sunny days. Cutting a cypress hedge is a job I avoid if possible. Beech clippings from today's hedge cutting were mixed amongst a pile of chippings from the walnut tree that was felled a few months ago. When decomposed, their final destination will be the vegetable garden.

Although a chaffinch or robin is never very far away, appearing at my side as soon as I walk out with a barrow or a hoe, two blue tits are now my most tame companions in the garden. A pocketful of peanuts has been essential in coaxing songbirds to become so trusting. Blue tits now feed from my hand, clasping the tips of my fingers with their curled, sharp claws for a fraction of a second as they deftly pick up fragments of nuts.

Planting and sowing had been taking precedence over other work this month, but now that the cold frame and seed packets are nearly empty, it is time to catch up. Grass cutting, hoeing, edging and weeding are required throughout the garden, but it has to be carried out in a systematic fashion.

I read yesterday that squirrels have a liking for strawberries. That reminded me to check the nets covering our strawberry beds in case blackbirds or thrushes had found their way in and then become trapped. This morning, as I crawled beneath the nets with string and wire, I noticed the first blush of pale red on one side of some of the lime green berries. I hope the family of four red squirrels that are regular visitors to the cottage windowsills for peanuts and birdseed will not be tempted in the coming weeks by the scent of ripe fruit.

The chauffeur and his wife celebrated their 40th wedding anniversary today. With the bishop's permission, they had invited around forty guests to Rose Castle for a party. The evening began with sherry on the lawn. Guests wandered round the garden before the meal, catching the last of the sun. Many commented upon the fragrance of roses drifting through the air; the perfume lingered in the still, sultry warmth of the evening. Later on in the dining room, between speeches, Jim and I played two sets of Scottish tunes. I thought it particularly appropriate, considering the setting and occasion, to begin with 'My Love is Like a Red Red Rose'. The version I chose was the original tune, generally unknown, but an extremely wistful piece of music with an attractive simplicity.

Shortly after eight o'clock this evening, I met the bishop in the castle yard and we set off on one of our regular walks round the garden. During the last two years, he has been intent on learning the names of plants and trees and keeps a notebook especially for gathering information on the subject. Towards the end of our walk, he mentioned that he would like a selection of new rhododendrons to be planted in the castle drive.

This evening, a group of around forty members of a local gardening club visited the garden. The west walls of the castle were illuminated by the low, summer sun. It is at this time of year, and during sunlit evenings, that visitors using the grass car park are fortunate to view the castle in one of its most appealing, gentle lights. Although the apothecary's roses are not quite in full bloom, their pink flowers and hedge-style of planting caught the eye of many of the visitors. The scent from yellow and cream flowers of *Lonicera* 'Graham Thomas', planted in the Bishop Nicolson garden, filled the evening air.

Last summer when some of the garden visits took place on damp, cold evenings, visitors lingered no longer than perhaps half an hour, but this evening everyone wanted to remain in the garden as long as possible. It was nearly ten o'clock before the last visitors left.

This morning I picked the first bowl of this summer's strawberries for the bishop's wife. The first few early potatoes were also lifted because I was fearful that two or three shaws of 'Romano' were perhaps showing signs of blight. Although slightly too early to be lifted, the potatoes would provide a meal for two or three evenings. The suspicious shaws were taken off to be burned, but on closer inspection, I doubt if it was blight at all.

The badger that regularly visits the moat woodland to dig up wild pignuts, *Conopodium majus,* has now turned its attention to bumble bee nests. A large excavation of dry soil at the base of a Scots pine in the woodland was a surprising sight this morning, but when we noticed a few bedraggled and disoriented bumble bees stumbling over the mound of soil, it soon became obvious what had happened. We see fewer bumble bees as each year passes. I am not sure what is causing their decline but it is a shame that a hungry badger is raiding the nests of the bees that are managing to survive in the garden.

It seems our young, two year old peacock has left for pastures new. At the beginning of the month, he disappeared for three days, during which time the bishop received a telephone call from a lady two miles away saying she had a peacock perched on top of her roof, and she suspected it might have come from the castle. The young peacock found his way back to Rose Castle of his own accord but is once again missing and this time has been away for over a week. This bird is one of the three hand-reared chicks orphaned by a fox and rescued by the chauffeur, and this is the first time in two years the siblings have been separated. One of the two remaining peahens is now sitting on three eggs in a nest that is well camouflaged amongst long grass growing around the base of a huge tree stump in the

paddock beyond the vegetable garden. For years, we have speculated on the possible species of this tree. Judging by the girth of the remaining stump, it must have been a magnificent specimen in its day.

Lower levels of rain throughout May and June have ensured a healthy potato crop with very few signs of slug damage. As I lifted 'Belle de Fontenay' and 'Yukon Gold', the dry, crumbling soil fell away cleanly from the potatoes, leaving the skins bright and fresh. A whole bed of 'Belle de Fontenay' was planted this year and most of these will go to the castle kitchen. 'Yukon Gold' is a variety I grow for baking in the oven, mainly for our own use. Even as early in the season as this, these yellow potatoes are exceptionally large and perfectly formed. It is amazing at this time of year how quickly the potatoes can increase in size. Tubers of 'Romano' remaining in the soil are now so much larger than those I lifted only last Monday.

Lettuce, rocket, coriander and young spinach leaves are abundant just now. As soon as one bed is completely cleared of potatoes, I sow more of these salad crops to ensure a succession of fresh young leaves. Such a wide variety can be grown quickly from seed at this time of year - it seems wasteful to leave any empty spaces and bare soil.

Yellow flag iris, *Iris pseudacorus*, is blooming in the fish pond. This old pond is now bereft of the water that once supported a healthy population of fish destined for the bishop's table. A small flight of stone steps, mossy but perfectly formed, lead from the top of the bank down towards the grassy floor of the pond. A barely discernible stream of water trickles in at the north side, keeping it moist enough for *Iris* and clumps of rushes. In drier areas of the pond floor, red campion and cow parsley grow up amongst the grasses. The sides of the empty pond are lined with stone, providing crevices for ferns that tumble down towards where the water should be. In his first few years here, Jim experimented with planting a few rows of potatoes in one corner; the soil proved fertile, and we had a fine harvest of early potatoes from within the sheltered environs of the pond walls.

We know there were other fish ponds at Rose Castle in the early fifteenth century, although we are not sure of their location. The 1649 Commonwealth Survey of Rose Castle mentions they were overgrown with weeds. In his botanical notebook, Bishop Nicolson records in 1703 that teasels were growing 'about the ponds.' Historical documents show that between 1735 and 1747, one of the

fish ponds was dug out and reinstated. At the same time an ornamental cascade was added, and in later years, the pond was surrounded by a 'palisade and iron work'. No sign of the palisade remains, but remnants of the stonework forming the cascade can still be seen quite clearly. Foxgloves grow amongst the stones of the old cascade, but we keep it free from all other plants so its outline can be pointed out to visitors to the garden. In the early 1900s, the pond was once again cleaned out and the island that we can see today was added, along with a bridge. The bridge has long since gone, but the island is now home to a thriving weeping willow, probably no more than thirty years old.

Whether used to stock the bishop's carp, or enhanced to become an ornamental feature, or both, the pond has inspired many bishops and gardeners during its long and varied life, perhaps because it is the only area of Rose Castle garden to have been documented in such detail through the centuries. At the moment, it is now a fairly neglected sunken garden, surrounded by yew trees and providing a natural haven for wild flowers, frogs, toads, dragonflies and songbirds.

A group of twelve ordinands staying at the castle for a few days spend many hours in the garden. The combination of warm, sunny days and the garden's full flush of flowers, lushness, scent and birdsong is irresistible. Idyllic and so tranquil, the garden offers the perfect setting for contemplation. Ordinands sit in the grassy woodland of the moat, beneath the scented blossom of the 'Rambling Rector' rose that scrambles through a damson tree in the orchard, or on the stone steps leading down to the white and purple border. Some are engrossed in books while others seem to be overwhelmed with the beauty of their surroundings. On my way to the gatehouse with a barrowful of potato shaws, I came across one ordinand lying stretched out on the grass beside the orchard border with his camera, intent upon photographing bees on the cushion of white blossom covering *Hebe buxifolia.*

This evening, as Jim and I were taking an early evening walk through the garden, the bishop came out to join us. We went to look at the newly opened, scented flowers of *Lilium regale* on their sturdy stems that have reached a height of over five feet. The scent from these large, trumpet-shaped flowers was particularly strong as it wafted across the lawns and upwards towards the open windows of the castle.

The bishop was curious about a small circle of uncut grass in the middle of the front lawn, not far from the gatehouse. The circle had been left uncut as an ephemeral feature; a piece of grass sculpture, carpeted with meadow buttercups shown off to full advantage by the surrounding, even texture of the green lawn. Last week, just as the buttercups were fading and we were considering cutting them, we noticed a solitary, slender spike of pink flowers rising from the middle of the circle. On closer inspection, it turned out to be a single plant of *Dactylorhiza*, the spotted leaf orchid. Although they are common on the grassy verges of Cumbrian roads, it is the first time we have found one growing at Rose Castle. In the hope that it may set seed and produce offspring in the same area of grass, the circle remains uncut.

JULY

The vegetable garden overflows with mellow lushness. Rows of leafy spinach, pods of young broad beans, the first courgettes, tightly curled parsley, loose and lacy coriander, lettuce in shades of green and bronze.

Strawberries have been memorable this summer. Warm, sunny days have ensured a daily supply of dark red, sweet fruit that looks so enticing as it lies beneath the nets ripening on a thick layer of straw. I pick the ripest fruit in the late mornings, by which time any residual dew has dried, but by late afternoon, more berries have already ripened and I could easily pick the same quantity again. It takes an hour each morning to work my way through the strawberry beds. The castle's long, wooden kitchen table is covered with bowls of strawberries, and there is still enough fruit to share between the cottages and the farm. Now that both our peahens are two years old and are sitting on nests, they have not been so troublesome, paying little attention to this year's strawberries.

In the borders, the late spring and early summer flush of growth is looking weary and a little unkempt. On lawns, areas of shallow soil are revealed by yellowing patches of grass where all moisture has been depleted. Some areas of the garden seem becalmed before summer's second burst of growth.

This week, I lifted nearly all the potatoes from the vegetable garden. Potatoes for eating are put into mesh sacks and stored in the small, cold pantry adjoining our cottage. Wooden plant boxes used for growing annuals earlier in the year are ideal for storing seed potatoes. These boxes were made at Haddo House garden during bitterly cold winters when hard-packed, frozen snow kept us confined to the potting sheds and boiler rooms. I brought them with me when I came here, knowing I would always treasure them. Every time I look at them or touch them, memories of these Aberdeenshire winters come alive, and I think of the visitors to the dimly lit, stone-floored potting shed, conversations in the Doric language of Aberdeenshire, and all the laughter, jokes, estate tales and old stories while the wood for the boxes was measured, sawn, and nailed together.

This year's crop of 'Salad Blue' has been abundant. I happened to be lifting potatoes this afternoon when the bishop was walking through the garden with his wife. I explained to him that 'Salad Blue' has dark purple skin and blue-purple flesh that retains its colour when boiled. He seemed amused at the prospect of ecclesiastical purple potatoes.

This variety has a lovely flavour, but the thought of purple potatoes does not seem to enamour many people. The chauffeur turned down my offer to try a few purple potatoes with his meal this evening. In case this variety is mistaken for a new, fancy, genetically modified potato, I always go to great lengths to explain it is, in fact, very old and traditional. But even so, the thought of purple potatoes still fills most people with unease.

The continuing dry weather has helped to keep slug damage to the potato crop to a minimum but has caused other problems, although only with one variety. 'Avalanche' has been infected with a severe infestation of scab, probably as a direct result of the warmth and dryness. I had to discard most of the larger tubers, but managed to salvage the smaller ones which, it must be admitted, tend to have

the most flavour. Three maincrop varieties will be lifted later: 'King Edward', 'Pink Firapple', and an unknown variety that was resident in the garden when we arrived, which I think may be 'Desiree'. I wish we could grow a larger selection of maincrops but slugs are an even worse problem here with varieties that have to remain in the soil for a longer time. 'King Edward' is grown mainly for baking, so the tubers need to be a good size before they are lifted. Last year's crop was badly damaged by slugs, but hopefully we will be luckier this year.

Trailing white *Lobelia* has adorned pots and containers to great effect this summer and is in full bloom at the moment. Some of the white is mingled with touches of blue – the result of seed that was not quite pure. A combination of white *Lobelia* with blue cornflowers rising through it was a last minute thought, but a planting idea that I will use again for pots in the yard.

High humidity and thunder-laden skies, heavy with rain that never falls, have now caused the strawberries to become susceptible to mould. Berries that are just forming become quickly blemished if they happen to be resting next to those that are already mouldy. As I do not use any form of chemical control for pests and diseases, the only solution was to spend a couple of hours crawling beneath the strawberry nets with scissors and a bucket, cutting off berries showing any signs of mould. This should prolong the crop for another week. Two bucketfuls of damaged berries were gratefully received on the compost heap by the blackbirds that are still successfully thwarted in their daily attempts to find a way in beneath the strawberry nets.

Blustery winds and skies the colour of wet slate still did not bring rain this afternoon but did provoke me into rushing around tying up any loose stems of broad beans, lilies and sunflowers. *Lilium* 'African Queen' is blooming in front of the office windows; dusky flowers in a wintry shade of yellow have an exquisite perfume.

One of the great joys of working in a garden every day is the opportunity to experience natural, ephemeral events, happenings that you would almost certainly otherwise miss. This afternoon's winds brought down a thick, snowy shower of white petals from the 'Rambling Rector' rose that grows through a damson tree. They floated down, carpeting the grass beside the herbaceous border and covering the wooden bench beneath the tree. I sat there for ten minutes or more, as the petals fell all around. Within an hour it was

all over; most of the loose petals blew away, scattering and disappearing across the orchard. I felt as if the garden had shared one of its special secrets.

The tame blue tits still follow me around the garden, knowing full well I always have a supply of peanuts in my dungarees pocket. The chauffeur has also spent a lot of time taming one of the male chaffinches that now taps on our bedroom window early in the morning, hopeful of a handful of birdseed as soon as we get up. A weekend of glorious sunshine and heat. It has been so warm that we have to water pots and hanging baskets twice a day. This evening, I watered all the rows of seeds I had sown during the past two weeks, fearing the heat and dryness would be preventing germination. This may sound like a lot of extra work, but in the warmth of the evening,

just as the sun was dipping below the wood on the hill above the castle, wandering around the vegetable beds with watering cans was a pleasant job. Although the heat has browned the lily flowers, it has encouraged a prolific flowering of night scented stock, which, by the time I was coming to the end of the evening's watering, had filled the air with its sweet scent.

A few years ago, Jim attached his tree climbing ropes to the top of the castle. As he slowly abseiled down on a harness, he stripped off the thick coat of ivy that had colonised most of the north wall. Although the ivy was healthy and, in many ways attractive, it had become too vigorous and invasive. The previous bishop's wife decided the ivy had to go when almost all the light was blocked from their bedroom window. Since then, the ivy has returned, reaching up towards the top of the castle and once again growing over the windows. Last week, we were asked if it could be removed. It is almost too hot to work in the garden just now in the afternoons, so the shade of the north wall was welcome. No ropes or abseiling this time, the chauffeur hung out of the top window and was able to scrape off the stems that had invaded the top of the building, Jim worked from a ladder in the middle section, and the young man who helps us in the garden dealt with the lower areas. As the ivy fell to the ground, I raked it up into heaps and barrowed it off to the bonfire. Meanwhile, the chaplain continued to work at his desk, even though this commotion of rattling ladders, tumbling ivy, shouting and merriment was going on at ground level outside his office window.

Two peachicks hatched yesterday. It is the first brood for the peahen, and she seems slightly unsure of the situation, not realising how much her chicks were suffering in the heat. Braving the sharp claws and beating wings of the hen, Jim rescued the chicks yesterday from the full strength of the sun and, followed by the irate mother, set them down in a shady area of the garden close to our cottage where they settled down and remained for most of the day. This afternoon the bishop took some photographs of them as they pecked around in the short grass for insects.

The thermometer registered 26°C in the shade this afternoon. Although it feels uncomfortably hot after midday, the early mornings are a delight. At seven o'clock, as I walked the geese down to their daytime enclosure behind the orchard, clouds of insects were illuminated in the low, morning sun. They hovered above the dewy grass, occasionally scattered by the swooping flights of chattering swallows. Time stood still and the castle stood in a pool of early morning pinkness.

The chaplain's office windows overlook a small border that lies to one side of the front door of the castle. Two Jacobite roses, *Rosa* x *alba* 'Alba Maxima', seem content to grow in this shady bed and provide a show of scented white blossom between June and July. In the past, between the roses, I have planted white foxgloves that I have grown from seed. Some still linger on as self-sown seedlings from parent plants, their whiteness retained by judiciously removing any young plants showing a flush of pink on their flower buds. About half the seedlings turn out to have white flowers. Apart from a few minutes in the early mornings and late evenings, this part of the castle remains constantly shaded. White spires of foxgloves and double, white roses stand out from the shadows. *Meconopsis betonicifolia*, the Himalayan poppy, is also planted in this border. Raised from seed last year, they may produce their first few flowers next May and, hopefully, will be as spectacular as those that flowered in our yard this spring.

The strawberry crop has come to an end, but is replaced with the first ripening tomatoes from the greenhouse. In the orchard, three 'Sanctus Hubertus' plum trees, planted by Jim during our second year here, have produced their first substantial flush of fruit. Branches are arching, heavy with the weight of ripe, sweet, purple plums. It is impossible not to make a short detour to the orchard at every opportunity to pick a few from the highest branches, and then savour the fresh, honeyed juices while standing in the damp grass and glimpsing Strickland's Tower between the trees. So far, there are only a few wasps to be seen around the fruit. In other years,

plums on the older trees have been ruined by thick clouds of wasps that descended upon the orchard at the first hint of ripening fruit. Yesterday, Jim cut the grass around the 'Sanctus Hubertus' to make them more accessible to anyone who would like to pick the plums.

In the vegetable beds where the potatoes were lifted, rows of rocket and Chinese cabbage are ready for use. Somehow, I sowed only three rows of garden peas in the spring. The pods are swelling and are now ready for harvesting. There is a great temptation to stand in the sun and eat the warm, freshly shelled peas straight from the pods; not all of them find their way to the castle kitchen. Next year, I must make sure I sow at least two whole beds - everybody loves fresh garden peas.

The hedge that runs along the south side of the garden, down past
the back of the orchard and parallel with the footpath to Rose
Bridge, is in the process of further reshaping after our work on it in
February. Jim has fashioned a couple of crenellations along the way –
a light-hearted reminder that this hedge is, after all, within the
grounds of a castle. These ramparts of hedging are causing a great
deal of speculation: already we have been asked why the hedge has
not been cut at the same level all the way along. He has also cut out a
porthole from the part of the hedge that faces the secluded seat
beneath the cherry tree. Now, anyone who sits at the wooden table
has a perfectly circular view across to the white blades of a distant
windmill and the top of Carrock Fell.

We decided to dedicate this week to the drive. Elder, laurel and rhododendrons have become wayward and overgrown, every month reducing the areas accessible with mowers. Yesterday we started at the top of the drive, cutting back sprawling stems of laurel, pruning rhododendrons, severing the corky stems of elder at ground level and removing some lower branches of trees. By late morning, we had two fires burning: one not far from the wooden entrance gate to the property, and another half way down the drive, close to the leaf mould amphitheatre. Unexpected, heavy rain later in the day failed to put out the fires but left all of us soaked and muddy. It was one of these days when, although it was very wet, it was too warm to wear a coat. In the midst of the downpours, the chaplain passed us and shouted a cheerful greeting as he strode out along the tarmac towards the castle. He had walked two miles from Dalston and streams of

water were pouring from his shirt, but rather than finding it an unpleasant experience, he seemed to be relishing his walk back to the office through the summer rain.

July departed with bottle-green dragonflies dancing through dappled shade between the trees in the woodland. Heart-shaped poplar leaves, grown lush and voluptuous from this summer's warmth and moisture, flutter languidly in a lazy breeze drifting across the bog garden. Fully ripened, purple-black plums are now dropping freely from the branches of 'Sanctus Hubertus'. Apples are tinted with shades of pink and red, and pears are losing their greenness to hues of amber and rust. Faded and tired, the flowers of early summer are replaced with the vibrancy of *Rudbeckia, Cosmos, Verbena, Echinacea* and *Salvia*. The few courgettes that remain unpicked have turned to marrows. Pods of peas and French beans hang from entwined stems. Late summer has arrived.

ONE YEAR LATER

This time last year, long, ripened grasses in shades of amber, beige and brown formed a glowing carpet of colour in the moat. Looking down into the moat today, the grass is lush and green. The arrival of a new mower in the spring meant we were able to cut the central area of the moat throughout the season. Long grasses and thistles still grow on the bank, providing a food source for wildlife and attracting as many goldfinches as ever. This afternoon, the scent of freshly cut grass filled the air as the mower worked through the moat. We are enjoying another heat wave with the temperature in the shade reaching 23° C according to my thermometer on the north wall just outside the door of Gardener's Cottage. High temperatures and dry, dusty grass do not always agree with mowers - the engine had to be switched off on several occasions to let it cool down. As soon as they were glimpsed, young toads were rescued from the path of the mower. These toads inhabit the base of the terrace wall, crawling into spaces in the ancient stone buttresses and moving out to hunt for their prey amongst the dense grasses. Toads are always highly respected here. We like to believe they help to keep slugs and snails under control.

When I heard that Cumbria was due to receive as much sun this week as some Mediterranean areas, I lifted all the onions and brought them round to the yard. They are now laid out in the sunniest spot, rapidly drying off in the August heat, their outer skins turning crisp and papery. This garden grows an admirable crop of large onions, and anyone passing through the yard on their way to the potting shed or our cottage never fails to comment upon them, especially 'Red Baron' with their glossy, dark purple skins.

Luxuriant, long, warm days begin without a hint of chill in the air and remain that way until late at night. A haze of heat hangs over the moat in the afternoons without even the slightest breeze to blow away the thistle down. Grass cutting and hedge cutting is carried out in the mornings so that the energetic work is completed by midday when the heat begins to make us less efficient. In the shade, the thermometer records a reading of 28° C. The south-facing windows of our cottage remain wide open all night and day. Sweet scents of flowers, cut grass, and the spicy aroma of sap from cypress and yew clippings fill every room. In the evenings, I sit outside our cottage, reading and writing until the last few bumble bees have departed from the lavender and the first pheasants have flown up to roost. If only every summer could be like this.

Yesterday, in the early evening, I lay on the grass in the orchard for a while watching the geese lazily perusing the low branches of the young apple trees. The old gander could select his apple by neatly pecking it off at the stalk, but the two younger geese approached the problem with less finesse by grabbing the branch in their beaks and roughly shaking it until an apple fell off. As I watched the butterflies and moths amongst the clover and grass, the geese wandered beneath the trees, finally spending some time eating the fallen plums before I walked them through the vegetable garden to their shed where they would be free from the danger of foxes throughout the night.

Two new guinea fowl that we bought at the Longtown poultry auction on Saturday are beginning to settle down. The auction just happened to take place on the warmest day of the year so far, but the guinea fowl did not seem to suffer during their journey back to Rose Castle in a slatted, wooden box the boot of the car. The new white fowl is wandering around freely with our two old, resident fowl. Not so sure of its new surroundings is the new lavender-coloured fowl that flew up into the cedar tree to roost last night and has yet to work up the courage to come down. We worry that the old guinea fowl may die through the winter – they must be at least seventeen years old – and we want to have younger birds already established in the grounds before that happens.

After such a long warm spell, the bog garden looked as if it might be less boggy than usual and perhaps dry enough to cut with the tractor mower. Underfoot, the ground felt quite dry and solid. This was bad judgement on our part. The wheels of the mower broke through the surface layer and began to sink into black mud not far from the gatehouse. Last night, we tried to lever it out of the mud using

wooden posts and a pinch bar, but it would not move enough to let us drive it out of the mud. This morning, when the chauffeur had returned from driving the bishop, he changed out of his suit, put on his overalls and came to help, but still the mower would not move. The farmer, busy with his cattle, noticed us in the distance having some sort of problem and offered to come over with his tractor and pull the mower out with a rope. After a few manoeuvres with the farm tractor, it was freed from the thick mud. The lady who is the house-keeper for the castle can remember clearly when this bog garden area was filled to the brim with water, just like a moat.

Due to the continuing warmth, late sowings of broad beans and peas are producing a heavy crop. During previous summers, I always hoped that we might benefit from later sowings, but a combination of

low temperatures and consecutive days of rain usually prevented the vegetables from developing fully. This is the first year we can say that late sowings of legumes have been successful. Yesterday, I sowed more lettuce, rocket and coriander into the large covered frame. In mid September, when night temperatures begin to fall dramatically, I will keep the frame covered. There should be a good supply of salad crops well into October.

This afternoon, we collected four more new guinea fowl from a farm near Wetheral. These birds are ten months old, each with identical markings of dark grey feathers speckled with white as if they have been caught in a flurry of snow. This latest addition to the Rose Castle bird population brings the number of guinea fowl to eight.

In the orchard, the first few greengages are ripe and ready to eat. Two old, gnarled trees are bearing their large, heavy, oval fruits much earlier in the season than usual. Young greengage trees, planted in 1996, produced their first crop of perfectly round, exquisitely flavoured gages last year. Strangely, they are completely bereft of fruit this year.

After I had taken the geese down to their shed this evening, I met the farmer walking up from the fields along the farm track. The first topic we always discuss when we happen to meet is the long-range weather forecast. While he is desperate for rain to make the grass grow for his cattle, I am happy with the thought that our dahlias, 'Italian White' sunflowers, ornamental gourds, pears and damsons will continue to thrive in this late summer warmth.

After a full day spent reshaping a yew hedge, Jim and I sat out in the garden until darkness fell, enjoying a glass of claret. Furry, brown moths fluttered around pots of night-scented stock. In the fading light, the silence of the evening was broken only by the forlorn, haunting calls of a pair of oyster catchers as they flew low over the gardens and quickly disappeared from sight behind the dark silhouette of the bishop's castle.

Rose Castle and its garden and grounds - a history

1217 When Carlisle is in Scottish hands, the government of Henry III writes to the Archbishop of York regarding the welfare of the Bishop of Carlisle, '...the bishop is in the utmost need, and hardly has where to lay his head'.

1230 Henry III gives the manor of La Rose to Bishop Walter Mauclerc.

1242 Bishop Walter Mauclerc receives a present of a pack of staghounds from Henry III.

1300 King Edward I and Queen Margaret visit La Rose.

1314 During a truce in conflicts between the Scots and English, Robert the Bruce's brother, Edward, stays for three days at the bishop's house at Rose.

1319 Bishop John de Halton restocks the fish ponds at La Rose after raids by the Scots. Twenty-four young deer are brought to restock the park.

1322 Robert the Bruce burns La Rose.

1336 Bishop John de Kirkby given permission to crenellate the bishop's manor at Rose.

1337 Scots return to raid Carlisle. They burn the bishop's manor at Rose, '...and everything on their way there'.

1346 Scots again burn the bishop's manor. 'It is unlikely that Bishop John de Kirkby or Bishop de Welton cultivated rose and lily, hollyhock and peony, for the ever-present foe to trample underfoot'.

1355 Bishop de Welton given permission to crenellate his dwelling at Rose.

1374 Bishop Thomas de Appleby excommunicates poachers. '...those sons of iniquity who had broken into his park of Rose and took his deer with dogs, nets and other engines...'.

1400 – 1419 Bishop William Strickland rebuilds Strickland's Tower and gives his name to it. An area known as 'Le Herber' is set aside for the cultivation of vegetables.

1462 Richard Neville, Earl of Warwick, stays at Rose Castle.

1480 'The inner court was paved with cobbles, and the outer court was occasionally strewn with dried peat broken into small pieces...the hall was strewn with fresh rushes'. Staff at Rose Castle includes a butcher, miller, baker, brewer, maltster and cook. A reeve looks after the tithe of geese. Apples, pears and plums grow in the orchard and around the castle.

1488 – 1489 Bishop Richard Bell builds chapel on first floor and adds Bell's Tower.

1522 – 1524 Bishop John Kite builds Kite's Tower and rebuilds east range of Rose.

1580 Bishop Richard Barnes assures Queen Elizabeth that during his incumbency 'timber trees' were not felled.

1616 Bishop Henry Robinson dies of the plague at Rose Castle.

1621 Mrs Milbourne, wife of Bishop Richard Milbourne, sends apples from Rose Castle orchard to Naworth Castle.

1642 Bishop Barnabas Potter dies at Rose; there is no successor at Rose until the Restoration of 1660.

1648 Much of Rose Castle and Strickland's Tower burnt by Parliamentarian troops during the Civil War. '...Rose Castle, the Bishop's best seat, hath lately the rose therein withered, and the prickles in the ruins thereof alone remain'.

1649 Rose Castle falls into Parliamentary hands. In the Commonwealth Survey it is noted '...the fish ponds about the castle are grown up with weeds...an orchard without the south and east quarter of the castle containing about three roods of ground...there are fine walks of oak and ash...the trees growing near and about the castle, being in number 120...'. The surveyors also recorded '...there is in the midst of the square of the aforesaid castle a very useful fountain which runneth continually and serveth the offices in the said house with water'.

1650 Sir William Heveningham buys Rose Castle and restores part of the west range using the mason Alexander Pogmire.

1660 Restoration of the Church of England, Diocese and Bishopric. Bishop Richard Sterne restores Rose Castle chapel.

1672 – 1675 William Thackeray carries out restorations for Bishop Edward Rainbow. A contract dated 28th January 1674 shows that £3.10s. was allowed 'for Wm. Thackeray's horse a year and an half, at grass in summer and hay in winter, with a Cowe-grass about 3 quarters of a year'. Lady Anne Clifford (Anne, Countess of Pembroke) presents a door lock inscribed 'A. P. 1673' to Bishop Edward Rainbow.

1676 John Twentyman, Bishop Edward Rainbow's gardener at Rose Castle, is invited to Brougham Castle to give advice on the gardens.

1684 Bishop Thomas Smith restores part of the castle and adds Smith's Tower using the amateur architect The Revd. Thomas Machell.

1700 Dovecot built for Bishop Thomas Smith.

1702 Bishop William Nicolson records lists of plants that are sent to Rose Castle from the Royal Botanic Garden, Edinburgh. He keeps detailed records of wild flowers he finds in Cumbria in his botanical notebook.

1715 Jacobite Rising. Flood water and high river levels prevent the Scots from raiding

Rose Castle.

1719 The son of Bishop Samuel Bradford writes, 'We rise about 6, breakfast and study till 11, dress and to prayers in our chapel, walk in ye gardens...'.

1730s Wells filled in. Old fish ponds dug out and a cascade added.

1745 Jacobite Rising. Rose Castle is the backdrop for the following story. After the capture of Carlisle by Prince Charles Edward Stuart, a party of Highlanders set out to attack Rose Castle. On arrival at the door, the attackers were informed that the Bishop's daughter had just given birth. The Highlander leading the attack then removed the white cockade from his bonnet, pinned it to the baby's clothing and declared the occupants of the castle to be under his protection.

1747 Extracts from a letter from the Bishop's servant about the desolate state of Rose Castle: '...Several windows being very Bad....Several Dores not fit to stand... the Rats are so very plenty...a ould painted oyle Cloth with very great hols in it...not a pot in the Kitchen but what was as Black with inside as with out...'.

1750s Bishop Richard Osbaldeston carries out repairs to the castle and puts coping on the garden walls. He also builds a new farm house.

1760s Strickland's Tower re-roofed by Bishop Charles Lyttelton. Improvements around the property include 'pulling down the old garden house on the bowling green'.

1770s A payment of £33.18s.1d. is made by Bishop Edmund Law 'to labourers carrying away rubbish and removing a mount, filling up and levelling the ground in the Hopgarth and converting the same into meadow or tillage'.

1780s The fish pond is cleaned out and the mud removed, the sides are lined with masonry, and the pond is enclosed with a palisade and iron-work.

1800 Bishop Edward Vernon brings shrubs from Scotland and Keswick for planting the borders which were 'raised in some parts by many cart loads of soil brought from the wood'.

1808 – 1827 Bishop Samuel Goodenough, member and first Treasurer of the Linnean Society of London, is a botanist and an enthusiastic gardener. Events are held in Rose Castle gardens, and the garden and surrounding land provide supplies for the castle. But the bishop writes, 'No one here knows the difference between a thistle and a sunflower'.

1828 – 1830 Bishop Hugh Percy rebuilds much of the castle to its present state with the help of architect Thomas Rickman. Percy's Tower is built.

1830 The road from Rose Bank to Rose Bridge is re-routed away from the castle.Gardens and outbuildings are restored.

1852 Strickland's Tower is fully restored by architect Anthony Salvin. Sir Joseph Paxton is commissioned by Bishop Hugh Percy to design and lay out terraces and rose gardens at Rose Castle, perhaps between 1850 and 1855, although the exact date is unknown. It is thought he also designs the Dutch garden – an area of intricate parterres and gravel paths situated on the site of the present-day orchard.

1871 Resident castle staff includes gardener William T. Palmer, aged 21, and gardener William Thompson, aged 15.

1881 Resident castle staff includes gardener Samuel Foster, aged 30, and under-gardener Samuel Peel, aged 20.

1887 Mrs. Gertrude Ring Prescott, daughter-in-law of Canon J. E. Prescott, visits Rose Castle during her honeymoon and writes, 'there are velvety lawns, terraces of flowers, grand old trees, vast greenhouses of peaches, nectarines, apricots, pine-apples, melons and grapes, the melons hanging in bags. It must take an army of gardeners to keep it so perfect'. Seven oak trees are planted near Rose Bridge to mark the occasion of Queen Victoria's Jubilee. They are planted in the form of a hexagram, with the tree in the middle planted by Bishop Harvey Goodwin.

1891 Resident castle staff includes gardener Samuel Foster, aged 40, under-gardener Robert J. Adams, aged 25, and under-gardener Charles Rutherford, aged 18.

1905 – 1920 Bishop John William Diggle and Mrs Diggle carry out garden improvements. Overgrown laurel hedges are removed and collections of ferns, clematis and rambling roses are planted. The fish pond is cleaned out and an island and bridge added. Yew and beech hedges are planted. The moat area on the west side is excavated and filled with water. Borders, rose beds and glasshouses are tended by Mrs Diggle and Mr Mutch, the gardener.

1921- 1939 Several Rose Castle staff write notes in pencil or leave their signatures on the interior walls of Strickland's Tower. William Storey, came April 1921; Allinson, head gardener, came Nov 192? -1925; Edward Victor Herdman, chauffeur, came May 26 1926; Fred Halliburton, finished Rose Castle 17th March 1934, started 1926, married Sept 9th 1939; snow 16/1/23; Rose Castle staff dance, 16 Jan 1933; Go for glass, bring cutter, ruler and tape; Irish Queen.

1942 – 1945 The bishop vacates Rose Castle in 1942. Rose Castle is used as a store by the RAF between 1942 and 1945. The garden and grounds become neglected but the orchard produces an abundance of fruit. Nurses and administrative staff from Carlisle Infirmary are invited to visit the gardens in the summer to collect fruit that is then made into jams and preserves for the patients in the hospital.

1952 Rose Castle is returned to the Church Commissioners who demolish the Victorian kitchen and construct a new south end. In the process a small, walled, south-facing garden area is created.

1955 – 1966 The bishop returns to Rose Castle in 1955. 'Bishop Thomas Bloomer drags the gardens back from wilderness status' and restores the main lawn. Mrs Marjorie Bloomer is a keen gardener and fond of growing roses and other flowers. She plants a wisteria in Kite's Tower garden in 1956. The outline of the Dutch garden is still discernible but it is considered too overgrown to restore and is returned to grass. The vegetable garden is expanded and new fruit trees are planted, some of which are grafted from remaining old trees. Lupins thrive on the east-facing terrace and create a spectacular display of blue and purple that is visible from the road near Rose Bridge. The old oak tree that 'the bishop took his hat off to' is still standing. Mr Storey, the gardener, known for growing and showing onions, decorates Rose Castle potting shed with his 'First Prize' certificates. After his retirement, his successor in the garden is Paddy Dalton followed by Bill Meek.

1966 – 1972 A crop of Christmas trees is removed from the moat. Henry Noblett is asked to visit the garden by Bishop Cyril Bulley to offer his advice on fruit trees that are dying. Honey fungus is found to be the problem. A watercress bed is made. It is recorded that the garden is kept neat, tidy and colourful.

1972 – 1988 Bishop William Nicolson's 1702 botanical notebook is published in 1981 under the title of 'A Seventeenth Century Flora of Cumbria'. Gardener Bob McCrone maintains a productive vegetable garden that supplies the castle. He also tends a flock of sheep in the moat. Gladioli and chrysanthemums from Rose Castle are used for decorating Carlisle Cathedral. Early daffodils planted in the drive are used for posies for Mothering Sunday. Bishop David Halsey's chauffeur, Sandy Gemmell, is responsible for grass cutting. Using a cylinder mower, he cuts ornate initials of Charles and Diana in the main lawn at the time of the royal wedding. After Sandy Gemmell retires, he is succeeded by Alan Scott in 1982 who lives in Chauffeur's Cottage with his wife, Helen Scott, who is employed as housekeeper for Rose Castle. Mrs Halsey recalls, 'Rose had a typical northern garden, mainly lawn with a few flower beds. The lawns were useful for garden parties. Japonicas grew by the entrance gate from which we made jelly'. Bishop Halsey's daughter, Mrs Jane Hasell-McCosh, writes, 'breakfast was often eaten outside in the rose garden and lunch eaten by the summer house'. When Bob McCrone retires, he is succeeded by Russell Elms, then Derek Groucher.

1989 – 1994 On Bishop Ian Harland's arrival at Rose Castle, chauffeur Alan Scott greets him at the front door with his bagpipes and ceremoniously pipes him into the castle. Bishop Ian Harland and Mrs Sue Harland enhance the garden, reducing in size the areas dedicated to vegetables and soft fruit, and planting many shrub roses. When gardener Hugh Stirling leaves, he is replaced by Andy Graham. Melanie Weston is appointed as gardener in 1991 and plants daffodils on the bank of the moat. Ernie Peacock is appointed as gardener in 1993 and plants the border beside the gatehouse and the banks of the bog garden. He designs and plants Mrs Harland's private little garden situated outside the kitchen door on the former site of the pigsty and chauffeur's garage. A white herbaceous border is planted on the east-facing terrace, and white climbing roses are planted against the east-facing terrace wall. With the help of the gardener, chauffeur, and the Hertherington family at the farm, Bishop Ian Harland keeps a flock of sheep that graze in the moat. Hens, geese and guinea fowl are also kept.

1994 Canon Dr. David Weston, Peter Strong and Ian Caruana carry out a small archaeological excavation between Strickland's Tower and the north wing of the castle. As a result of the excavation, Canon David Weston sets down a line of stones that represents the line of the west side of the east range of the castle that was demolished in the late 17th century. Pottery fragments, clay pipe stems, coins, jettons, musket balls, window cames and a bronze book clasp are found. Mains electricity is extended to Strickland's Tower. Doorway to Kite's Tower is reopened. New gates, designed by Canon David Weston, are hung on the gatehouse.

1995 – 2003 Jim Waugh is appointed as gardener. An area to the south of the castle, overlooked by Gardener's Cottage, is laid out in a formal fashion with small vegetable beds, box hedges and grass paths. Roses, bought by Bishop Ian Harland, are planted in the shape of a cross with rectangular beds between. This area, adjacent to Chauffeur's Cottage, is named after the rose and is known as the Apothecary's garden. A soft fruit garden is planted. The wooded area of the moat is cleared; fences removed, banks cleared of brambles, mature trees shaped and crown-lifted, young trees planted and a grass path mown through the woodland. Wooden benches are made and placed in secluded or sunny spots. Young fruit trees, including apples, pears, damsons, plums and greengages are planted in the orchard. The white herbaceous border is replanted with white and purple-flowered perennials. Jim Waugh is assisted by Bill Lightfoot who succeeds Alan Scott as the bishop's chauffeur in 1997. Janet Queen and Paul Silvester work in the garden on a regular, voluntary basis. On Boxing Day night in 1999, a very large, mature cedar tree on the front lawn to the north of the castle falls in gales. In a field to the west of the castle, a small woodland, including three *Sequoiadendron*, is planted in 2002. Most species of trees are chosen to echo the mature specimens already growing in the drive and grounds. Jim Waugh retires in 2003 and Janet Queen is appointed as gardener.

2003 - 2009 The post of full-time chauffeur is not renewed after 2004 and Janet Queen is responsible for grass cutting and garden maintenance. The old weeping willow by the gatehouse falls in storms.

2007 Lightening strikes a *Sequoiadendron* and mature pine tree in the drive. The pine is felled shortly afterwards. Henry Noblett revisits the garden and recalls his visit during Bishop Cyril Bulley's episcopate. Paul Silvester and Jim Waugh volunteer their help in the garden. Bill Strathern from Gretna is contracted to cut all the hedges. A collection of rhododendrons is bought by Bishop Graham Dow and planted in the drive and moat woodland. Mrs Dow requests that more rhubarb is grown. Two new beds are planted with crowns of rhubarb split from a variety already established in the garden.

2008 - 2009 Young fruit trees are planted in the orchard. Varieties of apples include 'Ashmead's Kernel', 'Lord Lambourne', 'Tydeman's Early Worcester', 'Cox's Orange Pippin' and 'Burgh Beauty'. Also planted are 'Victoria' plum, 'Opal' plum and 'Willingham' greengage. The east-facing, white and purple herbaceous border is reduced in width by half for ease of maintenance. In March, Bishop Graham Dow holds his retirement service at Carlisle Cathedral to which all the castle staff are invited. This is preceded by Bishop Ian Harland's memorial service in Carlisle Cathedral in February at which James Scott, the son of bishop's chauffeur Alan Scott, plays 'Highland Cathedral' as a lament on the bagpipes.

The Bishops of Carlisle with the year of their accession to the bishopric.

1	Athelwold	1133	35	Henry Robinson	1598
2	Bernard	1204	36	Robert Snowden	1616
3	Hugh de Beaulieu	1219	37	Richard Milbourne	1621
4	Walter Mauclerc	1224	38	Richard Senhouse	1624
5	Silvester de Everdon	1247	39	Francis White	1626
6	Thomas de Vipont	1255	40	Barnabas Potter	1629
7	Robert de Chause	1258	41	James Ussher	1642
8	Ralph de Ireton	1280	42	Richard Sterne	1660
9	John de Halton	1292	43	Edward Rainbow	1664
10	John de Ross	1325	44	Thomas Smith	1684
11	John de Kirkby	1332	45	William Nicolson	1702
12	Gilbert de Welton	1353	46	Samuel Bradford	1718
13	Thomas de Appleby	1363	47	John Waugh	1723
14	Robert Reade	1396	48	George Fleming	1735
15	Thomas Merke	1397	49	Richard Osbaldeston	1747
16	William Strickland	1400	50	Charles Lyttelton	1762
17	Roger Whelpdale	1420	51	Edmund Law	1769
18	William Barrow	1423	52	John Douglas	1787
19	Marmaduke Lumley	1430	53	Edward Venables Vernon	1791
20	Nicholas Close	1450		(Harcourt)	
21	William Percy	1452	54	Samuel Goodenough	1808
22	John Kingscote	1462	55	Hugh Percy	1827
23	Richard le Scrope	1464	56	Henry Montagu Villiers	1856
24	Edward Story	1468	57	Samuel Waldegrave	1860
25	Richard Bell	1478	58	Harvey Goodwin	1869
26	William Senhouse	1496	59	John Wareing Bardsley	1892
27	Roger Layburn	1503	60	John William Diggle	1905
28	John Penny	1509	61	Henry Herbert Williams	1920
29	John Kite	1521	62	Thomas Bloomer	1946
30	Robert Aldrich	1537	63	Sydney Cyril Bulley	1966
31	Owen Oglethorpe	1557	64	Henry David Halsey	1972
32	John Best	1561	65	Ian Harland	1989
33	Richard Barnes	1570	66	Graham Dow	2000
34	John May	1577			

Bishop William Nicolson's Notebook

The following two lists of plants were recorded by Bishop Nicolson in his hand-written, botanical notebook which remains in Rose Castle library. Mr James Sutherland, the supplier of the plants, was the first Regius Keeper to be appointed at the Royal Botanic Garden, Edinburgh.

November 19ᵗʰ 1703
Set in the Garden at Rose (and my wife's little Garden) the following Shrubs, sent from Mr Sutherland; Or, at least, so many of 'em as the Carrier brought to my hand.

> *Deep purple Lilac*
> *Dwarf Medlar*
> *White Beam Tree*
> *Rose without Thorns*
> *Yellew Rose*
> *Buck horn-Tree*
> *French Tamarisk*
> *German Tamarisk*
> *Sea Buck-Thorn*
> *White flower'd Lilac*
> *Mock Willow*
> *Upright Honey-suckle*
> *Wayfareing Tree*
> *Shrub Trefoil*
> *Early-flowring upright Honeysuckle of the Alps*
> *Late-flowring upright Honeysuckle of the Alps*
> *Dwarf Almond*
> *Sweet-smelling American Rasp*
> *Shrub St Johnswort*
> *Curran with Gooseberry Leaves*
> *Persian Jasmin*
> *White Pipe Tree*

March 24ᵗʰ 1703/4
Set at Rose, from Mr Sutherland –

> Ranunculus Lanuginosus grumosa radice. *Illyrian Crowfoot.*
> Chondrilla Viminea. *Twig branch'd Gum-Succory.*
> Clematis Pannonica. *Hungarian Climmer.*

Veronica erecta quadrifolia Virginiana. *Virginian Speedwell.*
Eryngium Mediterraneum. *Land-Eryngo.*
Aconitum flore ex albo et coeruleo variegato. *Party-colour'd Monk Hood.*
Chamaedrys Teucrij facie. *Mock Tree-Germander.*
Cynoglossum Creticum. *Hounds-Tongue of Candie.*
Papaver Pyraenaicum flore luteo. *Moutain-poppy with a yellow flower.*
Pulmonaria maculosa flore albo. *Spotted Lungwort with a white flower.*
Iris Gloriosa. *Proud Flower de Lis.*
Jacobaea Maritima folijs minus incanis. *Sea ragwort.*
Aster Virginianus Serotinus flore parvo albente. *Narrow-leav'd Virginian Star-wort.*
Telephium minus repens folijs deciduis. *Creeping Orpine.*
Ptarmica Matricariae folijs. *Feverfew-leav'd Sneezewort.*
Androsaemum flore maximo Montis Olympi. *Large flower'd Tutsan.*
Iris folio Gramineo. *Grass.*
Hepatica Nobilis flore rubro.
Ranunculus montanus folio gramineo. *Mountain-Crowfoot.*
Cortusa Matthioli. *Bears-ear Sanicle.*
Ranunculus folio plantaginis.
Absinthium maritimum Lavendulae folio. *Sea Mugwort.*
Chrysanthemum erectum Angustifolium Virginianum altissimum. *Virginian Corn-Marygold.*
Millefolium maximum flore albo.
Valeriana Alliariae folio.
Linaria purpurea odorata.
Aster Novae Angliae Latifolius paniculatus flore saturate violaceo.
Thlaspi Creticum semper Virens. *Ever-green Candy-Tufts.*
Aster montanus serotinus folijs subrotundis. *Late Mountain Starwort.*
Thalictrum Canadense Aquilegiae folijs. *American Meadow-Rue.*
Doronicum Americanum. *American Leopards-Bane.*
Aster Tripolij flore Latifolius. *Broad leav'd Starwort.*
Aconitum Serotinum flore coeruleo. *Late flowring Monkshood.*
Cortusa Americana flore squallide purpureo. *American Sanicle.*
Trifolium Acetosum erectum luteum Virginianum. *Virginia-Woodsorrel.*
Origanum folijs ex albo variegatis. *Party-colour'd Wild Marjoram.*
Origanum folijs ex luteo variegatis.
Flos solis radice perenni. *Perennial Sun-flower.*
Scabiosa Argentea Angustifolia *Silver-leav'd Scabious*
Geranium tuberosa radice *Bulbous rooted Cranesbill*

Seeds ordered for Rose Castle garden, January 2003

Annuals

Acroclinium 'Double Giant Mix'
Bidens ferulifolia 'Golden Goddess'
Centaurea 'Blue Diadem'
Cerinthe major 'Purpurascens'
Cleome spinosa 'Violet Queen'
Cosmos bipinnatus 'Purity'
Cosmos bipinnatus 'Dazzler'
Cosmos sulphureus 'Crest Lemon'
Eschscholzia californica 'Inferno'
Helianthus 'Italian White'
Helichrysum bracteatum monstrosum
  'Crimson Violet'
Helichrysum bracteatum monstrosum
  'Silvery Rose'
Lathyrus sativus var. *azureus*
Lathyrus odoratus 'Wild Form'
Lathyrus 'Old Spice Mixed'
Lathyrus 'Old fashioned Mix'
Limonium 'Purple Attraction'
Lobelia 'White Cascade'
Matthiola bicornis 'Starlight Scentsation'
Nicotiana 'Lime Green'
Nicotiana 'Avalon Bright Pink'
Papaver commutatum 'Ladybird'
Papaver rhoeas 'Mother of Pearl'
Rudbeckia hirta 'Rustic Dwarf Mixed'
Salvia horminium 'Claryssa Mix'

Perennials and Biennials

Cheiranthus 'Blood Red'
Dierama 'Blackbird'
Euphorbia mellifera
Meconopsis betonicifolia
Verbena bonariensis
Veronica virginica 'Alba'

Trees and Shrubs

Colutea arborescens
Colutea x media
Euonymus planipes
Liquidambar styraciflua
Picea breweriana
Pinus coulteri
Prunus mahaleb

Vegetables

Chard 'Bright Lights'
Runner Bean 'Scarlet Emperor'
Runner Bean 'Royal Standard'
Broccoli 'Claret'
Broccoli 'Romanesco'
Carrot 'Early Nantes'
Cauliflower 'Clarke'
Courgette 'Gold Rush'
Courgette 'Supremo'
Leek 'Musselburgh'
Lettuce 'Marvel of Four Seasons'
Lettuce 'Tom Thumb'
Lettuce 'Webb's Wonderful'
Mangetout 'Dwarf Sugar Sweet'
Mustard 'Red Gaint'
Onion Sets 'Golden Ball'
Onion Sets 'Red Baron'
Pea 'Hurst Green Shaft'
Radish 'Sparkler'
Spinach 'Perpetual'
Tomato 'Ailsa Craig'

Herbs

Basil (Lime) *Ocimum basilicum* var.
  citriodorum
Basil (Tree) *Ocimum gratissimum*
Coriander *Coriandrum sativum*
Parsley 'Afro' *Petroselinum crispum*
Rocket *Arugula*
Wild Rocket *Diplotaxis muralis*

Potatoes planted in Rose Castle garden, spring 2003

Avalanche
Belle de Fontenay
Brodie
Claret
Foremost
Harmony
Highland Burgundy Red
Karina
King Edward
Nicola
Osprey
Pentland Javelin
Pink Firapple
Ratte

Romano
Roseval
Salad Blue
Sangre
Shetland Black
Yukon Gold

Two unnamed varieties were also planted. One of those, with red skin, was growing here when we first arrived at Rose Castle garden. The other, with purple markings on the skin, was given to me as an unnamed variety. Altogether, twenty-two varieties were planted.

Wild flowers recorded in Rose Castle garden and grounds in 2003 and 2004

Achillea millefolium   Yarrow
Aegopodium podagraria   Ground elde
Ajuga reptans   Bugle
Alchemilla vulgaris   Lady's mantle
Alliaria petiolata   Garlic mustard
Allium ursinum   Wild garlic
Anthriscus sylvestris   Cow parsley
Arum maculatum   Lords and ladies
Bellis perennis   Daisy
Caltha palustris   Marsh marigold
Calystegia sepium   Hedge bindweed
Campanula rotundifolia   Harebell
Capsella bursa-pastoris Shepherd's purse
Cardamine pratensis   Lady's smock
Centranthus ruber   Red valerian
Centaurea niger   Hardhead
Chelidonium majus   Greater celandine
Circaea lutetiana   Enchanter's nightshade
Cirsium arvense   Creeping thistle
Conopodium majalis   Pignut
Convallaria majalis   Lily of the valley

Cymbalaria muralis   Ivy-leaved toadflax
Dactylorhiza   Spotted orchid
Digitalis purpurea   Foxglove
Dipsacus fullonum   Teasel
Epilobium angustifolium   Rosebay
  willowherb
Epilobium hirsutum   Great willowherb
Filipendula ulmaria   Meadowsweet
Fragraria vesca   Wild strawberry
Fritillaria meleagris   Fritillary
Galega officinalis   Goat's rue
Galanthus nivalis   Snowdrop
Gallium aparine   Goosegrass
Geranium pratense Meadow crane's bill
Geranium robertianum   Herb robert
Geum urbanum   Herb bennet
Glechoma hederacea   Ground ivy
Hedera helix   Ivy
Hieracium umbellatum   Hawkweed
Hyacinthoides non-scripta Bluebell
Iris pseudacorus Yellow flag iris

Lamium purpureum	Red dead nettle	*Rubus fruticosus*	Bramble
Lathyrus pratensis	Meadow vetchling	*Rubus idaeus*	Wild raspberry
Leucanthemum vulgare	Ox eye daisy	*Rumex acetosa*	Sorrel
Lotus corniculatus	Bird's foot trefoil	*Rumex acetosella*	Sheep's sorrel
Lychnis flos-cuculi	Ragged robin	*Scrophularia nodosa*	Figwort
Lythrum salicaria	Purple loosestrife	*Senecio jacobaea*	Ragwort
Meconopsis cambrica	Welsh poppy	*Senecio vulgaris*	Groundsel
Mercurialis perennis	Dog's mercury	*Sherardia arvensis*	Field madder
Mimulus guttatus	Monkey flower	*Silene dioica*	Red campion
Myosotis arvensis	Forget-me-not	*Sonchus asper*	Prickly sow thistle
Narcissus pseudonarcissus	Daffodil	*Stellaria holostea*	Greater stitchwort
Origanum vulgare	Wild marjoram	*Tanacetum parthenium*	Feverfew
Oxalis acetosella	Wood sorrel	*Taraxacum officinale*	Dandelion
Papaver rhoeas	Field poppy	*Trifolium pratense*	Red clover
Papaver somniferum	Opium poppy	*Trifolium repens*	White clover
Petasites hybridus	Winter heliotrope	*Urtica dioica*	Nettle
Polygonum bistorta	Bistort	*Veronica officinalis*	Speedwell
Potentilla erecta	Tormentil	*Veronica chamaedrys*	Germander speedwell
Primula veris	Cowslip	*Vicia cracca*	Tufted vetch
Primula vulgaris	Primrose	*Viola odorata*	Sweet violet
Ranunculus acris	Meadow buttercup	*Viola tricolor*	Wild pansy
Ranunculus repens	Creeping buttercup		
Rosa canina	Dog rose		

Birds seen in, or passing over, the garden and grounds of Rose Castle

This list was compiled by Bernard Landreth when he was living in Chauffeur's Cottage in 2005.

Barn owl
Blackbird
Black-headed gull (Several in grassy area of moat)
Blue tit
Bullfinch
Buzzard
Chaffinch
Chiffchaff
Coal tit
Collared dove
Cormorant   (Flying south)
Crow
Dunnock
Fieldfare
Goldcrest
Goldfinch
Goose (Pink-footed or Greylag) (Large group in 'V' formation flying south)
Great black-backed gull   (One or two with herring gulls)
Great spotted woodpecker
Great tit
Greenfinch
Grey wagtail
Heron (In small paddock beyond garden – looking for frogs?)
Herring gull   (Small and large groups fly north each evening at dusk)
House martin
House sparrow
Jackdaw
Jay

Kestrel
Linnet
Long-tailed tit
Magpie
Mallard
Merlin
Mistle thrush
Moorhen   (Lingered around the tiny pond at Gardener's Cottage)
Mute swan   (Pair flying north)
Nuthatch
Oystercatcher   (Grass area of moat and in field beyond)
Peregrine falcon
Pheasant
Pied wagtail
Redpoll
Redwing
Robin
Rook
Siskin
Song thrush
Sparrowhawk
Spotted flycatcher
Starling
Stock dove
Swallow
Swift
Tawny owl
Treecreeper
Wood pigeon
Wood warbler
Wren

The Pictures

All photographs are by the author.

189

Bibliography

Publications I consulted include:

Bean W. J., *Trees and Shrubs Hardy in the British Isles,* London, John Murray,1976

Brickell C. (ed.), *The Royal Horticultural Society Encyclopedia of Garden Plants,* London, Dorling Kindersley Ltd, 1996

Greuter G. (ed.), *International Code of Botanical Nomenclature (Saint Louis Code) 2000,* Germany, Koeltz Scientific Books, 2000

Hume, R. (ed.), *RSPB Birds of Britain and Europe,* London, Dorling Kindersley Ltd, 2002

Rait R. S. (ed.), *English Episcopal Palaces,* London, Constable & Company Ltd, 1911

Thomas, G. S. *Perennial Garden Plants,*London, J.M. Dent & Sons Ltd 1985

Tyson B., *William Thackeray's rebuilding of Rose Castle Chapel, Cumbria1673 - 75,* Transactions of the Ancient Monuments Society, 1983

Whittaker E. J. (ed.), A *Seventeenth Century Flora of Cumbria,* Surtees Society, 1981

Wilson J., *Rose Castle,* Carlisle, Thurnam, 1912

Janet Queen was born in Oban on the west coast of Scotland. After working in gardens in Perthshire, she studied horticulture for three years at the Royal Botanic Garden, Edinburgh.

Formerly a head gardener with the National Trust for Scotland, and on private estates in Northamptonshire and the Outer Hebrides, Janet now lives in Cumbria, northern England. As well as maintaining Rose Castle garden, she works as a garden writer, contributing regularly to magazines and newspapers. She is also developing her own garden in Lunigiana, northern Italy.

Acknowledgements

I am very grateful to Bishop Ian Harland and Mrs Sue Harland, and Bishop Graham Dow and Mrs Molly Dow.

Special thanks to Canon Dr. David Weston for his help, encouragement and suggestions. He dedicated time to researching historical information about the garden, gave me copies of relevant documents and photographs already in his possession, requested and collated personal recollections about the garden from people with close connections to Rose Castle, and then willingly read through my typescripts.

Bernard Landreth offered valuable guidance in the formative stages of this work and also provided the Rose Castle bird list.

Personal recollections of Rose Castle garden were supplied by:
Bishop David Halsey and Mrs Halsey
Bishop Ian Harland and Mrs Harland
Canon Dr. David Weston (former chaplain to Bishop Ian Harland)
Jane Hasell-McCosh (daughter of Bishop David Halsey)
The Venerable T. R. B. Hodgson (former chaplain to Bishop Cyril Bulley)
Carolyne Baines (former secretary to Bishop Cyril Bulley)
David Bloomer (son of Bishop Thomas Bloomer)
Helen Scott (former housekeeper to Bishop David Halsey and Bishop Ian Harland)

But the garden could not be as it is without:
Adrian Brown who keeps castle and garden walls from crumbling
Graham Dunlop and his knowledge of the property's plumbing, drains and water
Stephen Hetherington and the supplies of manure from the bull's shed
Paul Silvester who works voluntarily in the garden on Tuesdays
Joe Dias and the crack at morning coffee in Gardener's Cottage